Pivot

and

Accelerate

The Next Move Is Yours!

Dennis E. Gilbert

Printed in the United States of America.

North Charleston, South Carolina, USA

ISBN: 1493589822

ISBN-13: 978-1493589821

LCCN: 2013922770

Be strong enough to pivot and courageous enough to accelerate.

~Dennis E. Gilbert

CONTENTS

Dennis E. Gilbert

PREFACE

There are thousands and thousands of books on self-improvement, change, and creating success. Unfortunately when it comes to individual or business change and success, many people and businesses fall short of the requirements or expectations for lasting, impactful change.

Our world is changing. Because it is changing, people are looking to arm themselves with new tools and enhanced mind-sets that will allow them to pivot on their path while maintaining the inspiration and motivation to persistently overcome new challenges and adversity that they face in what is also known as *the new economy*.

Read this book to learn about pivoting, and how it is not the same as change, but incorporates change as one of the underlying principles of success. Read this book if you believe your path is fluid, or if you believe paths with rigid constraints have kept you from your success. Draw from this book a new or reinvigorated mind-set. Approach your life, your career, and your future by being strong enough to pivot and courageous enough to accelerate.

Dennis E. Gilbert

ACKNOWLEDGMENTS

As I prepared this section I couldn't stop thinking about the countless people who have impacted my life. I consider my life a journey, one that many times I planned and many times I didn't. Many people prepare to write a best seller, but many sell less than a few hundred copies. We often create opportunities and take chances—or we don't. I believe life is richer for taking chances.

I'm grateful to know and have influence from some of the world's most outstanding people. Most important are those family and friends who have stood beside me, lent a hand, an ear, or otherwise inspired me to do more, be more, and push for more. I'm thankful to be inspired by those who taught me that persistence, confidence, and focus can overcome talent when talent isn't working hard.

This work brings to life many of my values and beliefs for success. For everyone who has been part of my journey, thank you!

Dennis E. Gilbert

CHAPTER 1

PIVOT

To improve is to change; to be perfect is to change often.

Winston Churchill[1]

We have all heard time and again about the need for change. We hear about changing ourselves, changing our workplace, and especially about changing our economy. There seems to be a certain intensity associated with the word; some believe it is good, others believe it is bad. Perhaps our experiences shape this intensity: those who experienced success from change look forward to success, while those who faced unending challenges resulting in failure to change perhaps see mostly bad.

Pivot is different. It includes change, but suggests that change is part of our paths and that our paths are not always a straight line. I consider fluidity, adaptability, and strategy to be structurally part of the pivot process. As people, we can pivot too often, pivot too late, pivot too soon, or not pivot enough.

Pivoting is problem solving. Contrary to what the actions of many may indicate, avoidance does not solve problems. Staying stuck or doing the same thing over and over again will most likely yield the same or similar results. Continuous and repetitive problems lack pivot. Avoiding problems sends a message of acceptance and the status quo. If you really want a different outcome, you're going to have to pivot. Trying something different may not be the same as doing different things. Remember that doing the same old thing isn't safe; in a changing world it is the riskiest place to be.

Sure, pivoting is about action, but it is more about mind-set. Mind-set is easy to talk about, hard to develop, and can never be faked. More than just thinking confidently and boldly, mind-set is also about how you perceive things. Perception is what determines the outcomes of your mind-set. When you see obstacles and hurdles in your path, your mind-set may signal avoidance or hesitation. If you see those situations as opportunity, your mind-set may signal action.

Action has never been more critical for creating results. Many people would quickly agree that everything in the world around them changes. In business seminars I've often asked, "Is everything around us changing?" I always get well beyond a majority quickly shooting their hands in the air or nodding their heads to signal agreement. Logic suggests that if everything around us is changing, one of the riskiest options for any person or business is to stay the same. Business failures are cloaked by the status quo. Kodak, IBM, and even at one point Apple Computer, Inc., experienced extreme setbacks and failures by not making timely changes.

The status quo often feels easy, safe, and historic. It may be based on tradition, image, and brand. On the surface it appears logical. A keep-doing-what-works attitude may be prevalent but it is this mind-set that starts trouble. This mind-set makes both individuals and businesses completely miss opportunities in narrow strategic windows.

A willingness to pivot is more than an attitude; it is a mind-set. Forces of change may cause us to pivot, but individuals with the most success engage early, ahead of the bell curve, and so have greater chances for success. What may need changing the most is the way you think. Sometimes you already know the answer. The problem may be facing it.

Pride and stubbornness drive people to work very hard, but facing a force of change that never quits goes far beyond pride, hard work, or being stubborn. Ask a blacksmith—if you can find one—or your local newspaper, or Blockbuster, LLC, about facing forces of change. Persistence will lead you to success, but likely not without pivoting.

In our minds we sometimes question if our persistence will pay off. It is this uncertainty that creates a distraction, which may cause us to hesitate, ultimately causing our worst fears to come true. Limited distractions are part of the pivot mind-set, because while inclusive of change it is more about a persistent focus. Distractions tend to show up with another unwelcome guest, their favorite cousin: regret.

People often worry about regret too late. It seems many people and businesses believe settling for less will make them feel safe and happy; it works initially until they discover their safe and happy has shifted to resentment and envy. Chances are they failed to pivot, and pivoting is about learning. It's OK to fail when you try. You'll learn something. It's not OK to fail to try. You'll learn nothing except regret. People and businesses that are on the path for positive change are different; they find themselves settling for nothing.

THE DIFFERENCE BETWEEN PEOPLE WHO DON'T BELIEVE AND THOSE WHO MAKE IT HAPPEN BOIL DOWN TO ONE THING: LIMITATIONS.

Limitations may be restrictions that your mind sets based on past experience or other input and feedback. For many businesses and people, what they accomplished was viewed as impossible—that is, until someone did it. The difference between people who don't believe and those who make it happen boil down to one thing: limitations. Limitations tell some people to shut down, back off, or retreat. Others see limitations as challenges that they haven't tested. Pivoting tests the limits of your ability and competence. You many never know how far you can go until you've been tested.

I believe there are guiding principles that help people get on track and stay on track as they create the lives, careers, or businesses they desire. Principles vary from religious, to moral, to ethical, etc., but one thing remains consistent: people. You will always face the somewhat unpredictable nature of people. Sadly, people who make poor choices—who live their lives with a lot of regret, envy, and unhappiness—often strike out, strike back, and try to limit your success. I believe you have two choices. The first choice is to live the life they want you to live. This can include reacting to their fear of separation. If you are a friend in their networks, your growth may threaten their happiness out of fear you may leave. The second choice is to live the life and create the future that you want, not the future that is limited by others' beliefs. When you make the commitment to pivot, you make a move that is yours!

What do you believe in? Do you have to see it to believe it? Empirical evidence is critical in research, a court of law, and science, but people who are innovators and those who are creating a positive future have to dream it before they actually see it. This is a sharp contrast from conventional "seeing is believing" approaches. Sometimes we have to believe in things that we can't see. People who focus on "seeing is believing" tend to live their lives in the past, dwelling on their mistakes and failures. Others tend to live their lives believing that what you focus on is what you get. They create their futures by pursuing dreams, making positive change, and by spending little or no time reliving past negative experiences.

In other cases, some people have small dreams, seldom take action, and believe they are stuck at the expense of others' success. They have a label for these successful people and businesses: lucky. I guess that means that good luck and good fortune come to those who dream big, take risks, and see challenges as opportunities—including those who pursue their visions by being honest, using their heads, and working from their hearts.

Jim Collins and Morten T. Hansen wrote about luck in their book *Great By Choice*. Their research in this area is important, and their findings are astounding. They explain that "Luck happens, a lot, both good luck and bad luck."[2] It seems consistent with their findings that how people or businesses manage their luck—both good and bad—somehow determines their future. This is not surprising; with sarcasm I might say, "Amazing!" Even more interesting and revealing in their work is the idea that some people anticipate the possibility of a stroke of bad luck here and there; they plan for it, prepare for it, and manage it as effectively as possible.

Do you have a spare tire in your car? Those prepared to manage a bad-luck event probably do.

Some believe luck doesn't matter much, and still others have little or no belief at all. People often search for the crystal ball that will allow them to see into the future. In many ways your future is very easy to predict. What you do today will be in the past tomorrow, and at the same time, tomorrow also represents your future. So your future is not really that hard to predict—it's what you're doing today.

Pivoting is certainly not free of challenge. Both people and businesses often reach a plateau or get stuck. Being stuck may mean their focus has slipped, their level of discipline or commitment is off, or they simply are not persistent enough in their efforts. Accountability is critical, and those who don't take responsibility for their decisions, actions, and behaviors are—or will likely become—stuck. Feeling that they can't do it, they often try to break others' momentum and limit their chances for success.

They may have told you it couldn't be done, it isn't worth the effort, the price is too high, or the timing is off. In some regards they could be right, but only if you allow it. Those who are committed to their goals and dreams feel differently. To them giving up feels like everything, and regarding price, they believe nothing costs more than regret. I believe something should break; you should break free of their negativity, poor judgment, and self-limiting beliefs.

CHAPTER SUMMARY

Pivot may be viewed as a process, but it also requires focus, a positive outlook, and courage to walk a path that sometimes seems full of wrong turns, dead ends, and, worst of all, ridicule. The people who try nothing, gain nothing. That is what pivot is all about: reaching for more, recognizing both what works and what doesn't, and never allowing the fear of failure or success stop them from the pursuit.

Success is not measured with material things. Success occurs when you dare to dream, challenge yourself, risk something sacred, and come out better than before. I believe people who achieve more do it intentionally, through persistence, focus, and with self-confidence. They face challenges and take responsibility for their decisions; they never quit. They never stop. They only pivot and accelerate.

Dennis E. Gilbert

CHAPTER 2

PLANNING

Planning is bringing the future into the present so that you can do something about it now.

Alan Lakein[1]

If you have never heard of Alan Lakein, you should know something. He wrote a very popular book titled *How to Get Control of Your Time and Your Life*. It is reported to have sold over three million copies.[2] This is important not because his book sales will impact your progress or success, but because it makes it clear that many people, perhaps several million, seek more control over their time.

This chapter is not about time management, priority management, or even about delegation—although planning, and perhaps more importantly the execution of a plan, could involve all three. Most would quickly agree that planning is important. Some may argue that they simply go with the flow, but those who are achieving their goals are most likely planning to succeed.

One danger that comes with planning is chronic planning, or planning that never moves into the execution phase. Fear, perfectionism, or lack of confidence could hinder your desire to get started. Of course you have to start to finish, and that means that execution is even more critical than the plan. Planning needs to be ongoing and continuous. The ability to pivot from an original plan is not a sign of failure in the plan, but a sign that you are planning not to fail.

Sometimes people think about planning their next move, but people who accomplish their goals are already creating their next plan.

HAVE YOU?

Would have, could have, and should have—these are common thoughts for people who look back at their lives with regret. Many people make difficult choices in their lives. Some chose not to finish college or pursue a career. Some made choices about family matters: where to live, who to marry, or about children. So many people sacrifice so much for others.

Creating your future success is not about rearview mirror reflections so much as it is about change, risk, and forward thinking. It is not so much about what you did or didn't do yesterday as it is about what you will do today and tomorrow. People don't become successful with a defeated mind-set. They become successful through forward thinking.

Have you thought about what you want to finish this year? what you want to get started on next year? or where you see yourself in two, three, or even five years? Have you made a plan for making things happen, making a difference, and forwarding progress?

REACHING FOR SUCCESS

Recognizing factors that limit your success can help you discover new levels of achievement. One of the most common limiting factors is setting the bar too low. Not to be confused with establishing goals that help you achieve small wins that build your confidence and position you to keep reaching for more, setting goals with a vision of safety in mind will almost always limit the level of success you achieve.

Are your goals fuzzy? Are you unsure of your next moves or where you want to go? Are your true role models seemingly beyond the level of success you feel you can achieve?

If you answered yes to any of these questions, it may be time to rethink your strategy. Being realistic with your next move is smart; setting yourself up for easily achieved goals that are not ambitious or don't cause you to reach will result in low output, thereby limiting successful accomplishments.

Are you reaching for more?

LOST GROUND

I admire the passion I see from people who try to overcome their weaknesses. This is noble; it builds character, and in some cases creates success. What I find puzzling about this conviction is what they sometimes give up.

What are you good at? What are your natural talents and abilities? What comes easily to you that you can capitalize on?

Too many people self-assess, discover weaknesses, and expend enormous amounts of energy trying to compensate by working on weaknesses when they should be thinking more about enhancing their strengths. Suddenly, right before their eyes, they discover that their effort has only marginally improved the weakness. The far greater tragedy is that they have "lost ground" on their strengths. In some cases, their overall effectiveness is now less.

Have you been losing ground?

OFTEN WE ARE TAUGHT TO FIX THE WEAKNESS, BUT THE EASIER AND MORE SUCCESSFUL PATH IS TO FOCUS ON STRENGTHS.

Losing ground is not a desirable outcome for most people. Often we are taught to fix the weakness, but the easier and more successful path is to focus on strengths. You can do this by understanding what you are already good at. Similar to how you have come to recognize your weaknesses, it is simply the opposite mind-set.

What do you love to do? Chances are, you are good at that. What sometimes seems easy or perhaps even boring and not intriguing to you? Perhaps you are good or very talented at that. What comes naturally?

Honest self-assessment will help guide you. It doesn't hurt to get some advice from trusted family and friends, but be cautious how you pursue that advice because they may choose to be very kind about your abilities as compared to brutally honest. You need honest feedback in order to obtain the best impact.

Consider asking them, without any leading discussion, to tell you in a few simple words what they believe are some of your strengths. This should be easy for them; strength is good and likely they will see no reason it would hurt your feelings. Do not lead them by saying something like, "I think I'm really good at managing other people, do you agree?" This of course leads your inquiry and makes them uncomfortable if they do not see or agree with your self-reflection.

When you truly understand your strengths and can be honest with yourself about creating your goals and vision, then you must remember to find the right balance—a balance of focus on growing your talent with some effort, but not a focus on fixing your weaknesses. A focus on weaknesses is likely a focus for failure. Worse yet, you'll be even more discouraged because you tried very, very hard, but came up short. It is about balance; don't lose ground.

BLESSINGS, FORGIVENESS, OR NEITHER?

Do you take risky action and then seek forgiveness if it doesn't work out? or do you always ask for blessings before you launch? This may be one of the best debated discussion subjects outside of politics or religion.

People sometimes wonder how other people get away with so many things. The answer may be that they take risks. Keep in mind I'm not talking about illegal activity, or improper moral or business ethics, I'm talking about a little bit of healthy risk-taking.

Life and our choices often involve risk. Critically evaluating the pros and cons of any decision can sometimes help you choose wisely. Sometimes, well, you just have to take a risk.

Here is what I believe: for decisions or choices where you can afford the opportunity cost, but cannot afford or strongly dislike the cost of inaction—take a risk. If you have critically evaluated your circumstance, you'll often find that neither blessings nor forgiveness are required.

PERSISTENCE AND AUDACITY

Recently I've been posting on my blog and social media channels about being average. Average is OK. If that is your goal, and you obtain it, you've achieved success. Despite this, it seems to me that many people don't want average. Average may imply settling for mediocre.

When you think of average you have to consider your data set. In other words, what people or what things are you including in your calculation of average? An average professional athlete is already in robust company; many people would be thrilled to be in that crowd. An average Fortune 500 executive is already in an elite crowd, and many people would be thrilled to be there. What is in your average?

I'm inviting you to dream—dream big. It is a simple formula: the more audacious your dreams, the more you discover. Through your persistent and relentless pursuit you learn more about yourself and discover your strengths. You may discover a new path, one that you never even considered.

Dream audaciously and discover your success through persistence. If you don't dream and you don't try, you won't get there.

GREEN THUMB

I live in Pennsylvania, and from mid-April until very early in June, hobbyist and professional farmers gear up their green thumbs and visualize their yields. Planting seeds in fields is analogous to planting seeds for personal or business growth.

A farmer cares for his seeds; he tills the land, waits for the right timing, and plants the seeds. Once they are planted, the farmer has a vision for his emerging crop. He has faith and hope for the best weather conditions. He watches over his field, cultivates the land to limit weeds, watches for bugs, and worries through a few bad storms. After several months he starts to harvest his crops.

Personal and business growth is very similar. You have to care for and plant the seeds. This may be marketing your products or services, reaching out to your contact network, or further developing relationships with clients or customers. During and after planting your seeds, you must have a vision of the desired harvest (outcomes), and you must cultivate (continue to network, market, advertise) and watch for bugs (quality, competition, customer satisfaction) while also being aware of the economic climate or other threats. After several months you review your progress, compare it to the vision, take note of any necessary adjustments, and prepare to enjoy your harvest.

To get the best yield, ask yourself:

- What seeds am I planting?

- What is my vision for the harvest?

- What will I do to cultivate my fields?

- What opportunities are emerging?

- What are the threats?

Perhaps you have a green thumb after all. I'm thinking of green for good luck, or green as in money. Do you have a green thumb?

THE RIDE

Persistence in achieving your success is not only about reaching the destination, it is also about the ride. Make no mistake, the destination is important and represents achieving both short- and long-term goals, but you likely spend the most time on—and have the most vivid memories of—the journey.

Timelines and milestones are markers on the journey. The achievement of goals comes and goes as you continue to reach for more and discover your ability to obtain excellence. Reaching each successive destination, you may become addicted to plotting your course, then embarking on the journey, and ultimately reaching the destination.

While destinations may shift and change, and come and go, one constant is that you are on a journey. You may spend days, weeks, months, or even years on your journey.

Enjoy the ride!

BALANCED PLANS

Some people (and businesses) plan and plan and plan. The trouble with that logic is that they're still planning. Almost no one will argue that planning is important. In fact, many people would likely agree that a lack of planning creates a plan that will fail. The real problem is the inability to act on those plans.

Intense and prolonged planning can sometimes lead to procrastination to start. People can become infected, not with a carefully laid-out plan but instead with a paradoxical logic that subconsciously leads them to think that if they never actually start their plan then the plan cannot fail. As crazy as it seems, this logic has limited individuals and businesses alike. They continue on a nonstop journey of planning.

Continuous planning is a good idea, but only when it is balanced with action. Continuous planning invites change, something many people and businesses struggle with. Individuals and businesses who have balanced plans, execute those plans, and can pivot as required to succeed, are the ones with the best plans.

If you are not ready to take action and find yourself struggling with the launch, keep this in mind: while a plan that doesn't start seems unable to fail, never starting is not success. Instead, it represents failure.

Find the balance.

HESITATE TO LAUNCH

Sometimes it is not the idea—it is the execution.

Having a great strategy is just plain smart. Individuals and businesses typically spend a great deal of time planning. Nearly no one will argue that strategic planning is a bad idea, but, like most things in life and in business, you must have the appropriate balance.

Perfectionists want it right; they absolutely can't stand the idea of something not being perfect. Sometimes, in their pursuit of perfection, they simply fail to launch, or they miss narrow strategic windows because of their hesitation or unwillingness to get started.

LIKE A SEESAW WITH PEOPLE ON ONLY ONE SIDE, THEY ARE STUCK AT THE BOTTOM.

Individuals and teams who strategize and assume reasonable risk by launching their plans and making adjustments to fine-tune them typically discover more success than those who never leave the drawing board. Like a seesaw with people on only one side, they are stuck at the bottom. They have good intentions but no balance.

TIME—TRAGEDY OR STRATEGY?

It seems like there is never enough time. Believe it or not, one of the most common frustration points that I hear from individuals, even those in high-ranking positions, is that it is hard to balance or manage their time. Time management sounds simple, but is it?

The concept of time management is pretty straightforward; in practical application people get frustrated quickly. There are several main points that I always urge people to consider when they think about their time:

- You have to spend your time on high-return or high-value items whenever possible.

- You should be as strategic as possible, not as tactical as possible.

- There is probably not time for everything; you must prioritize.

High value and high return are the name of the game. There will always be low-value items that occupy some of your time—eliminate and simplify (and delegate) where possible. Many people describe their job as "firefighting," which means they use a tactical approach in which whatever develops or pops to the surface gets the attention. Bad move. Think and plan strategically. Sometimes this includes planning for the unplanned. Priorities will tend to unveil themselves, but you have to carefully analyze high-value and high-return items.

Managing your time doesn't need to be a tragedy. Think strategy.

REAL TRAGEDY

There is no shortage of people watching, judging, and trying to limit the success of others. Something is different for them: they lack the energy, commitment, and courage to create a new breakthrough for themselves. As a result they would sooner spend their energy trying to limit—or worse yet, sabotage—someone else's life experience.

Envy drives these people. They want to keep everyone as close to the bottom as possible. They would sooner share in misery and prevent accomplishments for others than offer any good advice or favors for those they view as one step ahead. It seems strange, and perhaps even unbelievable, but it is often true.

Their advice may be: don't try it, you'll fail.

What they are really expressing is that they aren't able to put it together for themselves. They find it easier to try to limit those around them instead of putting in the energy and effort required to do something great. If you asked them about their goals, they would probably say they have none, or they will offer a story of misery and sorrow followed by why it doesn't make sense to dream.

It's tragic, perhaps, but the real tragedy is not the infectious mind disease they are trying to spread. No way. The real tragedy is when you halfheartedly approach your mission, when you allow self-limiting beliefs to slow or halt progress—or worse yet, when you have no plan or goals at all.

Turn tragedy into triumph.

You know you can, but you also know the next move—it's yours!

CHAPTER SUMMARY

Plans are plans, or are they? Perhaps nothing is more important than having a good strategy. Like many things in life, planning—whether personal or professional—can be pictured on a scale as a continuum. On one end of the continuum you have those who never plan; they claim that spontaneity is the real energizer and question why they should plan. On the other end of the continuum you have those who are in a chronic state of planning. That is, they never execute their plans; they are permanently stuck in the planning phase.

Continuous planning is good, as long as there is execution along the way. Timelines and milestones should be part of the process. It is at these critical junctures that you see the need or the opportunity to pivot. The concept of pivot is what makes planning the most valuable. You have to check to tell when you are on course or off, achieving or not. The best part is that the process is fluid. You allow for the necessary changes to take place in order to shape the future you desire.

Balance your plans with action, and build in enough flexibility to allow for the pivot.

Dennis E. Gilbert

CHAPTER 3

OPPORTUNITIES

Business opportunities are like buses; there's always another one coming.

Richard Branson[1]

Opportunities have to be spotted to be seized. The trouble with many opportunities is they are never recognized or seized. Reasons for lack of recognition are plentiful, but one of the biggest culprits is human behavior. Many people live their lives in the rearview mirror, always looking back, trying to steer to their futures from the road behind them.

If opportunity presents itself while we are too busy focusing on the past, we will pass the opportunity to improve our future. Sadly, this very process creates more rearview mirror driving because we start to only see opportunities after they have passed. Then our hindsight makes the image of what could have been very clear. This further promotes more rearview driving, because by now many people have conceded to the idea that they just aren't lucky.

According to Jim Collins and Morten T. Hansen, we all have about the same amount of luck. It is how we manage both good and bad luck that has the most impact on our future. In their book *Great By Choice*, they wrote, "The critical question is not 'Are you lucky?' but 'Do you get a high return on luck?'"[2] If you wait for luck to create opportunities, you are going to miss many.

It seems that we either find or create opportunities. Economic woes always cause the opportunity environment to change, but the key is that they still exist. Blacksmiths, typewriters, and corded telephones may have very limited opportunities, but within each of those areas new and different opportunities have developed. Sure, there are still some of all three in existence, and they play a role in our society, but certainly none of them would likely be considered to create a cutting-edge opportunity.

Opportunities come and go; we often describe this as the windows of opportunity or strategic windows. One problematic area for windows of opportunity is that they are conditioned by our imagination, innovation, or the lack of both. People searching for solutions, as opposed to identifying problems, tend to uncover more opportunities. They think critically and innovatively and, as a result, create opportunities where onlookers saw nothing.

CRITICAL THINKERS ARE ALREADY ASKING WHAT'S NEXT; OTHERS ARE LIKELY SAYING NO, NOT YET.

You have to ask yourself or your business what you see for your future. Critical thinkers are already asking what's next; others are likely saying no, not yet. The trouble is they believe they are waiting for the right time—a time that never comes, or that comes too late. They have already missed it.

Opportunities emerge more often than most people realize, but they are disguised as challenges and appear cloaked in risk. Believe it or not, many people turn down good opportunities.

I believe you have a choice.

You can turn down, turn away, or turn over opportunity, or you can recognize it. Now it's your turn.

BEING AVERAGE

Reaching for more is how we continue to grow. We develop, we expand, and we improve. We pay a price for reaching for more: the price of discipline, of sacrifice, and of what we sometimes label as the "opportunity cost."

People measure by averages, such as the average price for gas, the price of an average dinner out. Some people even buy an average home or car. People reaching for more are not content with average.

Everything has a price, but for those who won't settle for less, for those who want more, for those who create their own path and achieve their success, the price to pay is less than the alternative—being average.

ACCOMPLISH SOMETHING BIG

As the year 2012 drew to an end, for some there was a tension in the air. This tension was caused by an unknown future. Yes, the Mayan calendar was never developed beyond the winter solstice, December 21, 2012. This five-thousand-year-old calendar stopped "counting" after this date. While many never gave it a second thought, some were planning parties for the end of the world. This could have been a big deal.

Like the Mayan calendar, opportunities don't just happen; we create them. If we want to accomplish something big, we have to think big, dream big, and put our plan into action. Sounds easy, but is it? Here are two things I notice about people or businesses that are successful:

1. They remain optimistic about the future and look for positive, growth-oriented opportunities.

2. They take chances and risk more. Simply put, they accomplish more because they risk more.

It is never too late to start creating future opportunities. Persistence and audacious goals will help you to accomplish something big!

ESCAPE, NIGHTMARES, AND PASSION

A secluded beach, a mountain resort, a ski trip, a boat excursion, or Walt Disney World. Everyone needs a break every now and then, but what if you made your life so great you didn't need to escape?

Let's face it: downtime is important—for everyone. A getaway vacation can make a tremendous difference in your emotional well-being and allow you to recharge and see things more clearly. Every day we need both activity and rest. The same is true for the bigger picture we call life.

Here is what I believe: You have to work hard, very hard. You have to work smart, very smart. People who work hard and smart have passion. They probably have some passion for what they do, are successful, and get some enjoyment from their job.

Some people create and live their dreams. They love what they do, and they do a great job. Others, well, they are always trying to escape.

What is your passion: living your dream or escaping your nightmare?

FRUSTRATED DECISIONS

Agitated, anxious, and angry, we sometimes feel pressured to make a decision. Decisions and choices are part of our everyday life. We decide what clothing to wear, what to eat, and in many cases what will make up our day.

Making decisions when we are frustrated or anxious may result in unfavorable outcomes. Decisions give us opportunities, and opportunities involve risk. Our assessment of risk often results in fear. Fear may cause us to hesitate, which may result in missing an opportunity in a narrow strategic window.

WHEN WE ARE STRESSED OR PRESSURED INTO DECISIONS, WE SOMETIMES MAKE CHOICES THAT HAVE UNFAVORABLE OUTCOMES.

Good decisions take time. It may take only a few seconds or minutes, or it may take hours, days, or more. When we are stressed or pressured into decisions, we sometimes make choices that have unfavorable outcomes.

Remember that in some cases a decision to do nothing is still a decision.

What will you decide today? Choose wisely.

PEOPLE IN ACTION

Sadly, I often encounter people who are not on their path to success. They often start conversations with excuses or blame for why they are not already successful. Granted, our world economy is not stellar at the moment—we do have to face that as a reality—but there are still many opportunities for those who are willing to take risks, dig deeper, and make sacrifices.

Some people are waiting. They talk about what they want to do and what they will achieve. Unfortunately they are making excuses. Unless they change their outlook, they will become the people who are only dreamers. There is nothing wrong with dreams; in fact, they are an important part of visualizing our futures. However, action is what gets you results.

People in action create their own futures. They face reality and make decisions and choices that position them for success. They may discuss the realities of the economy, mismanaged businesses, and trendy changes that affect their futures, but they are different because they waste very little time worrying about what will not work. They have one focus—creating their success.

What does this all mean? You have a choice. You can be only a dreamer and talk about what could have, should have, or would have happened, or you can be a success by facing reality, taking risks, and making sacrifices.

Are you waiting, or are you a person in action?

WAITING

Opportunity cost is a common term used in business. People talk about the opportunity cost of attending meetings, making client visits, or even attending a conference or workshop. It seems that everything people do has some opportunity cost associated with it that isn't always about money.

Missed opportunities are expensive and the cost may be hard to measure. Missed opportunities could be not being there when your child hit a home run, scored a touchdown, or made a goal. In business they may occur through a networking contact you failed to make, faulty customer touch points, or your availability when a special client needs your attention. Your career and future are also affected by the choices you make based upon opportunity cost. People sometimes say "timing is everything," but when it comes to our success, waiting for the right time may be the wrong thing to do.

Here's how this shakes out. Many people wait for opportunities to come to them and often experience a very high cost while being unsuccessful. Successful people spot opportunities emerging and in many cases create them. The big difference for those who experience success is that they are not only disciplined and persistent, but they never wait.

What are you waiting for?

HANDS IN POCKETS

In the early 1980s I was called to interview at Pennsylvania State University for a part-time position in one of their engineering departments. After meeting individually with a number of different people, taking a tour of the facility, and hearing a very thorough explanation of the job, I had a strong feeling they were looking for someone different.

My final discussion was with a kind, stern, and brutally honest man. As he started to walk me toward the door, he gave me some advice. He said it was evident I was enthusiastic about the job and that I interviewed well; however, they were looking for someone with a different background and different vision for their future endeavors. I wasn't surprised. I'd felt it coming.

We shook hands. "One more thing," he said. "The next time you interview somewhere, don't walk around or stand with your hands in your pockets. It gives the impression that you are not ready to work." Shocked but accepting, I thanked him for his advice.

The message I want to share is one that has stuck with me for nearly thirty years. You won't achieve success by walking around with your hands in your pockets.

CHANCES

Actions speak louder than words, or so the saying goes. Taking chances is part of engaging in your pursuit of new or different opportunities. Sometimes you feel like you know it is the right move—it just feels right. Other times you perceive a signal and label it a gut feeling. Taking a risk on a perceived opportunity still involves risk and requires you to make a choice.

When you have the awareness to identify opportunity, I believe you have two choices: (1) you can follow it, or (2) ignore it. The chance you have been waiting for may be right before your eyes. Most paths to success are evolutionary processes, building on one circumstance at a time. This leads to more opportunities—or fewer, depending on your choices.

Some people make choices to become great; others become great at never making any choices.

PERFECT OPPORTUNITIES HAPPEN OFTEN, BUT THEY ARE DISGUISED AS CHALLENGES AND LABELED AS WORK.

You have a choice to take a chance. Taking chances is a natural part of achieving your success. Do nothing and you get nothing. It is time to turn chances into good choices and choices into more chances. Perfect opportunities happen often, but they are disguised as challenges and labeled as work.

Do you believe in chances?

I believe that some opportunities just happen, and others are created. One thing they all have in common is they typically don't come around twice.

CHAPTER SUMMARY

It is opportunities that really matter, but many claim that they never have any. More likely, they fail to spot them, or when encountering them they quickly dismiss them as not a good opportunity.

Fear, hesitation, and self-doubt represent just a few of the barriers most people experience. If an opportunity cannot be found, it should be created. Creating opportunity is easier than most believe. Like finding humor in difficult situations, the same can be true for opportunities. You have to learn to think differently, see circumstances or situations differently, and develop an "eye" for recognizing or creating them.

People are constantly innovating new products. It isn't uncommon to hear someone say, "Why didn't I think of that?" You didn't think of it because you weren't looking for or creating the opportunity. It involves a different mind-set: being curious; focusing on solutions rather than agonizing over problems; or simply recognizing that when something isn't working well, there must be an opposite opportunity.

Opportunities happen often. The difference for those who are successful is that they take them or make them. Everyone else—they're still waiting.

Dennis E. Gilbert

CHAPTER 4

CHANGE

I have noticed even people who claim everything is predestined, and that we can do nothing to change it, look before they cross the road.

Stephen Hawking[1]

Do you want to start a conversation? Bring up change. So many people talk about change. They are quick to cite the good, the bad, but mostly the ugly. Change gets people excited. Most businesses quickly realize that if they want something to change, they need to figure out how they will assemble and align the masses. They often call this buy-in.

Buy-in is critical for successful change, but many people are not sure how to obtain it. My experiences with executives, middle management, and even frontline supervisors tell me that while buy-in is destined for the buzzword bingo card, beyond that things are fuzzy.

Of course, many will cite communication challenges as a precursor of failure to change, and it is true that communication is critical but also the need is obvious. What is not so obvious is the question of how to obtain buy-in. Buy-in is created by shared experiences. These might include people working together, communicating together, and finding success or failure—you guessed it—together. So business leaders developed the concept where they let it be their idea. But does it work? To some extent yes, but it isn't so much about their idea as it is about their sense of belonging and value. Sure, having great ideas is important, and if managed properly, they can dramatically improve efficacy. A component that creates self-esteem and self-confidence is a good thing.

Ownership is the word sometimes used to describe the value of belonging. Yes, people tend to manage change better when they feel some sense of control over their fate. Yet others believe fate is best left in someone else's hands. Still others believe that their destiny is predetermined and regardless of what happens next it is what is in the cards. The pages of this book could be filled with subject matter related to what is contained in this single paragraph, but that would be another (different) book.

Individual change, whether personal or professional, also requires careful management. Many have the desire to change; they talk about it and start something, only to revert to old habits quickly. The typical argument is that they didn't want it badly enough, so they let things slip. However, individual change goes well beyond desire. Individuals often need to be their own coach. Their vision of transformation is sometimes hard to detect. After numerous failures they may opt to discount and disregard change as soon as the word comes up. This adds to the organizational dilemma of individuals possessing low tolerance for change.

Change is important. Change is critical. Change must be managed. And of course, effective change requires buy-in. Whether working with individuals or businesses, people must buy in, recognize the need, commit, feel ownership, and have or share vision. The change must also be a good idea. As you'll read throughout this chapter, change needs commitment and transitioning. Successful change requires trust, patience, and time.

NOT FAIR!

People often have great questions during workshops. To be honest, some of them are very challenging to answer from a generalist point of view. Recently I have noticed a common theme to some of the tough questions. This theme appears to be related to "bad bosses" talking down to employees.

It just seems so unfair—people in power flexing their muscles and controlling the outcomes in what may be described as a bully approach. Many people are looking for the silver bullet or golden nugget that will correct this absurdly wrongful act. I have some reactions to share, but none of them are easy. Here is what I believe:

1. You likely won't change their behavior, but you can adjust your reactions.

2. People are different, and difference means diversity. Therefore, look for the good in this person.

3. You have choices. If you choose to stay and accept the less-than-enjoyable, focus on the

good and keep moving forward. Reliving past negative experiences will not help your cause now.

It all comes down to choices. It seems that everyone makes sacrifices, but what is important for each person is willingness to accept their sacrifice and not be resentful toward themselves or other people.

It may not be fair—but you have choices.

YOUR BIG BREAK

Lots of people are waiting for their big break. Frustrated, angry, and blaming everyone but themselves, people often tell me about how they are less because someone else got lucky, received gifts, or knew the right people.

In this case the bad news and the good news are the same. Those people or situations don't own you, you own you. Consider this:

Luck: Some experts' research reveals that we all have about the same amount of luck. Some is good, some is bad, but what you do with the luck you encounter is what makes the difference. A good-luck opportunity that isn't seized isn't worth much. A bad-luck situation that doesn't result in learning and adjustment isn't worth much, either.

Gifts: Similar to luck, your success is conditioned by what you do with the gifts you receive. We all have talents and abilities or receive gifts (a tie, flowers, money). What you do with what you have or receive results in changes in your attitude or life.

People: Expanding your network if you want success is never a bad idea. Reach out to someone new, someone different, someone who interests you, and someone who doesn't.

Some breakthroughs happen quickly; some take more time. Some may be the result of a lucky opportunity seized, some through actions created by gifts, and some through the people we know.

If you want positive change, here is the best news of all: you own your next big break.

PICK THREE

Some people believe good luck happens in a series of three. Others believe bad luck comes in threes. Some find ways to accomplish their goals in a series of three steps or action items, and still others have three excuses for their lackluster success.

Bad news: Some people limit their success by being locked in to a mind-set filled with negativity, cynicism, and unfavorable outcomes. They set themselves up for limited accomplishments, limited vision, and poor performance.

Good news: Successful people think differently. They believe they have control over their fate; they make confident choices. They visualize positive outcomes while creating promising futures. Their confidence is reflected in their presence. The people around them feel their passions while witnessing their successes.

Make today the day you start with a fresh commitment to your goals. So pick three. Pick three things that will make a positive difference to your future and start now.

Having trouble getting started? The first thing you need to pick is *you!*

HATE CAUSES CHANGE

Hate feels like a strong word. It is often used with little or no thought about its sometimes aggressive stance. However, being assertive and perhaps aggressive about creating positive change is a good thing. Here are a few examples:

- People hate being out of shape, so they start exercising.

- People hate seeing only the negative, so they get positive.

- People hate their earnings potential or job, so they change it.

Seems like a very clear pattern to me. Hate causes change. People sometimes buy in to change efforts because they hate the thought of the alternatives. I don't know about you, but when I really don't like dealing with hate, I change it.

What are you going to change?

SAFE PLACES

We know that things change; people talk about it often. What they don't talk about is what they are doing to change. The status quo feels like a safe place for many. It represents their comfort zone.

In our personal lives, we may be able to get away with the status quo or doing things that feel safe. For example, we may order the same food at a restaurant, in part because we like it and in part because we know it is a safe choice. We may shop at the same store, in part because we know the locations of each item, but also because it is comfortable and safe.

If you are one of the many who feel safety in the status quo, have you considered the risk of staying the same? Is there a risk? In your career or in your life beyond work you should be thinking more about breaking down barriers that lock you in to the status quo. What is your safe place: the status quo or change?

In a world of constant change, the riskiest place to be may be in a place of no change at all.

STICKING POINTS

Persistence is often noted as the key to reaching your next goal and achieving success. It has been said that people give up just before they achieve their next big break or discover and tap into great opportunities. I believe it is not about doing more of what you are already doing; it is about trying a new tactic or different approach.

Here are two short examples:

The boss: An employee always expresses dissatisfaction to the boss immediately after receiving assignments he is uncomfortable with, and the boss seems to listen but nothing changes. The employee tries a new tactic of scheduling a meeting with the boss and coming prepared with both issues and possible solutions. The boss, no longer assuming he is just complaining, agrees to try some of the suggested changes.

The store owner: A pizza shop owner is confused about why his business is slowing, despite great feedback from those who dine in. He gets common complaints and watches people struggle while trying to carry out their pizza because the doors to his fabulous shop open inward instead of outward. He changes the way the doors open and notices fewer dropped pizzas, fewer complaints, and happier customers.

People who remain persistent while also trying new approaches to accomplish their goals often discover newfound success. Move past sticking points by changing or trying something new, not by just doing more of the same.

CONTINUOUS IMPROVEMENT

Many businesses become fixated on concepts related to quality control, process improvement, and reducing waste. They spend significant percentages of their total budgets chasing these improvements. They love the buzz and cannot get enough of talking about TQM (total quality management), and more modern examples such as lean manufacturing, kaizen blitz, 5S, and Six Sigma.

These are noble, important, and valuable, yes, but at what cost? Everyone wants quality and value. Businesses know the importance of waste reduction, controlling energy costs, and buying high-quality raw materials at the best possible price.

Success, or the lack of it, has a great deal to do with mind-set. A mind-set of quality control, cost reduction, value, and customer satisfaction is fantastic. Unfortunately, the price of some of these cultures often creates a mind-set that is reluctant to innovate, change, or consider other alternatives.

I could make an educated guess that anyone who is responsible for these processes in their business would be willing to argue or debate that there are not any trade-offs. This is exactly why I am making the point. They often state continuous improvement, but they discourage contributions for new ideas, processes, or methods.

The idea is that they change until they achieve extremely limited or zero failure, then freeze and do not ever do things differently. Don't get me wrong; I support the idea of quality control, continuous improvement, and reductions in operating expenses as well as raw materials. I support all of those ideas, but the philosophy needs to recognize that when you make some of these concepts the culture of your business, trying to change that mind-set may become the biggest obstacle in the path of your future success.

REPETITIVE CHOICES

Persistence is what typically makes the difference for people who achieve success. However, persistently making the same type of choice, or attempting to solve problems in a flawed style, can result in a continuance of undesirable outcomes. Undesirable outcomes often lead to blame.

MANY OF THESE ARE REALITY, AND FACING THAT REALITY IS SOMETIMES DIFFICULT.

It's easy to place blame—blame to other people, circumstances, government regulations, and of course, the economy. Many of these are reality, and facing that reality is sometimes difficult. However, blame will not change your situation, and repetitive patterns of poor choices can lead to lower levels of self-confidence.

To be successful you have to make good choices. If success has been evading you, and you're not on the path that you should be, or you're not moving at an appropriate pace, it may be the result of poor choices. Change your approach, change what didn't work, and learn to make better choices.

What is worse than a poor choice? Not learning from it, and allowing history to repeat itself over and over again.

Learn to repeat patterns of success.

WORKPLACE HARMONY

In the workplace, people make choices about participation, learning, and commitment. These individual choices often result in the collective success of the department, team, or the entire business. When groups of people get this right, the end result is maximum output and collective drive to achieve the business's mission.

Business leaders often use buzzwords to emphasize key points for maximizing their intellectual capital. You may hear things like:

- buy-in

- synergy

- teamwork

- strategic alliance

- harmony

Employees sometimes develop a love-to-hate feeling for these buzzwords; however, the words are not the problem, it is the actions of all employees (including the "leaders") that make the difference. Empty words or words utilized without the appropriate corresponding actions are what sometimes create the turnoff rather than the turn-on for action.

Workplace teams need to work well together. People in businesses with solid workplace relationships are likely businesses that are maximizing their intellectual capital. These businesses have discovered and incorporate at least three things:

1. A connection with each other and the business.

2. They feel the purpose, and they are working passionately.

3. They have the desire and ability to work in harmony.

This should be simple—right? Is your workplace harmonized?

GET SMART—ADMIT IT

Feeling a sense of accomplishment and taking pride in your past achievements may be a great way to build self-confidence. Everyone should spend some time reflecting and assessing where they have come from and, more importantly, where they are going. This is not only practical, but smart.

People are often very knowledgeable about a certain thing or talented in a particular skill. They are very dedicated, and they are persistent as they pursue their dreams and achieve their success. Some reach a plateau and once there, they can't figure out how to get beyond what has become a sticking point.

They are limited by dreams that keep them small, by fear, or sometimes by their own capabilities. What worked to get them where they are now may not be the same thing that they need to take them to the next level.

Are you stuck? Are you smart? Dream audaciously, face reality, be persistent, and hire or outsource the help that you need. You have to be both willing and able to admit it and move past it, or be forever stuck.

Getting help is smart; it's not a matter of pride.

STAY SMART

A popular question from people I interact with is, "What if I can't achieve the success I desire? When should I give up?" Some may think the appropriate reaction would be to say never! While persistence is critical for your success, sometimes we have to know when to change course.

Here are three (of the many) examples of situations that may suggest you alter your course:

1. Your product or service is not innovative.

2. Your product or service was once in great demand but now has become obsolete.

3. You are aware of a financially (or spiritually) more lucrative opportunity that interests you.

Persistence is paramount, but you cannot do the same thing over and over again and expect different results. You cannot chase ridiculous dreams that are clearly not things you can accomplish. In many cases only you can make this assessment.

Dream big, be persistent, stay committed—and most of all, stay smart.

CHAPTER SUMMARY

Change may be considered to be synonymous with the word pivot, and in some ways I would agree; however, pivot is much more than change. It incorporates the fluidity of strategy that allows continuous improvements instead of a specific focus that just changes an event or circumstance.

People have been known to bellow in the halls of their businesses or the vast expanses of their manufacturing facilities, "Change is good!" or "All change is good!" Countering that, we may hear, "We've never done it that way," or "We've tried that before; it just doesn't work." Failure to change has left a bad taste in many mouths. Additionally, the status quo feels very safe.

Let's not forget about processes or practices that limit opportunities for innovation or growth. Many businesses push forward with quality standards, citing buzzwords such as TQM, Six Sigma, and other process and quality improvement ideologies.

These practices are of course good, but at that the same time they instill the idea of no tolerance for change. Anything outside of the very fixed process they have outlined, documented, and live by according to an industry standard is the ideological version—and therefore bad. Yet they try to obtain buy-in for change. Culturally, that is a paradox.

Not all change is good, and change for the sake of change is typically not recommended. Most importantly, though, change is happening all around us. Single-handedly trying to stop progress, innovation, ease of use, or anything low-cost, free, or otherwise emotionally exciting probably will not work. Individuals and businesses alike need to change.

Change can't happen soon enough for most. While one business hesitates the other capitalizes. Changing on the upside of the bell curve representing the life cycle of a product or service is smart, and you are much more likely to experience success. The competition is smaller, the margins are greater, and you get the distinct and well-proven benefit of the curve.

CHAPTER 5

CONFIDENCE

We gain strength, and courage, and confidence by each experience in which we really stop to look fear in the face...we must do that which we think we cannot.

Eleanor Roosevelt[1]

Confidence may be the single biggest factor in achieving the results you desire. We know confidence when we see it. When we feel it, there is something in the air that inspires us to do more. What could be better when this feeling is so highly contagious?

People sometimes ask about confidence. What is it, how do you get more of it, or do you show enough already? Our confidence may be built, or destroyed, by a variety of factors. In simple terms, there are two primary factors affecting confidence: self-esteem, and self-efficacy. Having more, or less, of either factor conditions your level of self-confidence.

Confidence is built. It is a collection of memories, inspiration, and passed tests, either real or imagined. A focus on wins or successes as compared to failures or shortcomings will have a significant impact on your confidence. Too often people focus on the shortcomings instead of the successes. Building on each accomplishment, no matter how small, will lead to more confidence.

Confidence is fragile. Take public speaking as an example. Many people have a big fear of public speaking. Understandably, this fear is very common. Numerous people tell me that one time they had a bad experience, and they could never do it again. So initially they had enough confidence to try, but when not completely successful they decided to never try again. I promise you, public speaking is not always easy, but managing your self-confidence and fear can make an enormous difference.

It may be more about fear than about confidence. If fear is more dominant than your confidence, you may choose a different activity that causes less fear. Yet fear is typically developed from learning experiences.

Also consider confidence that is based on task or environment. In some tasks we are very confident, while there are others we would never try. In some social or business settings we may feel very confident but in others, not so much. Following this logic, it would seem true that our good and bad experiences drive confidence.

Confidence is hard to beat, and that is why this chapter is critically important. If you don't believe in yourself, your team, or your business, no one else will either. Confidence is about belief, and it develops from a positive replay of vision that turned into success. Imagine that you can, visualize yourself as successful, relive that positive approach, and see yourself in the positive outcome. Often that is what you will achieve. Unfortunately, the complete opposite is also true. You have a choice. Choose confidence.

BELIEVING IN DREAMS

We are often conditioned for who we are or what we become based on beliefs we carry in our heart. Successful people believe they will achieve success long before they actually do. Many act surprised at their success, but perhaps it is an expression of humility.

People reaching for more should remember that they become what they believe. If they believe they can reach the next sales goal, achieve the next rung on the corporate ladder, or exceed their last personal-best performance, then they are much more likely to achieve it. In contrast, if they feel like they have little chance, set self-limiting goals, or listen to envious comments from others with unfulfilled dreams, they likely will achieve less.

Believe in dreams. If you know it in your heart and believe it in your mind, you can make your dreams come true. I'm a dreamer, I work from my heart, and I believe—do you?

LABELS

What makes the single biggest difference between those who achieve and those who concede to defeat?

Their minds!

The first place we start losing our momentum, losing ground, and halting our progress is in our minds. Sometimes we have some help with self-defeat; it comes from labels that we allow others to place on us. Sadly, friends, siblings, parents, teachers, and co-workers sometimes tell us that we can't, when in fact *we can.*

Don't allow negative labels placed on you by others to slow you down, limit your progress, or shatter your dreams. Don't listen to labels telling you that you are not good enough, are too young, too old, too skinny, or too heavy. Don't let the thought that you are undereducated or lacking experience slow you down or hold you back.

Instead, label yourself with positive thoughts, such as "I am an achiever. I'm smart, strong, attractive, energetic, motivated, and can create or do anything I push hard for, and I will pursue life with passion. Since I'm good and persistent, I will make it happen."

Pick your own label!

CONFIRMATION OF LABELS

If you consider labels to be a reality, then you should also consider why, how, or when labels get attached to you.

Let's start with *why*. People often learn or remember by association. They hear a name or see a face, and they remember it by associating it with another stored memory. People tend to do this either out of self-protection, positive interest, or some other desire.

How: Seeing is often believing, and what they see with their eyes—what they hear or even smell—can create a label of you. They associate you with another memory and add you to that list, or in some cases you may represent the start of a brand-new list.

When: People are nearly always scanning their environments and making choices or decisions about other people. This is especially true in social settings when they meet someone new. It is an ongoing process. Even someone familiar can be evaluated and reevaluated by others with similar or changing labels.

While some labels are good—and you may want to adopt these labels—others are negative and work against your success. Here is what I believe. You have two choices:

1. Confirm their label.

2. Prove you are not their label.

Good labels may motivate and inspire you; they let you know you're on track. Negative labels make your journey tougher; they challenge your self-confidence and, unfortunately, can create self-limiting beliefs.

Remember—you have two choices!

AVOID ACTION ANXIETY

Do you have an overwhelming fear of taking action? Do you have action anxiety? Action anxiety is the label placed on your fear to make a choice or get moving toward the pursuit of your success. Symptoms may include the inability to decide, extreme hesitation, or reliving (over and over again) past negative experiences.

The good news is that with hard work and a specific focus you can overcome action anxiety. Three things that you can do right now to minimize the effects are:

1. Focus on past successes.

2. Believe in yourself.

3. Take some reasonable risk.

Focus on making choices or taking action based on your past successes, no matter how big or how small.

COUNT SUCCESSES

Have you ever wondered what starts the fearful process of losing? You work hard, attempt to make the best choices, but sometimes you still end up losing ground in your progress. Accomplishing your goals and creating your success is never easy. The first place you start to halt your progress is in your mind.

The first moment you start to believe that you can't—when you should be thinking that you can—is when you significantly slow down or perhaps halt your forward momentum. It is amazing the control that the power of thought has over your outcomes.

THEY HAVE LEARNED TO FOCUS ON BEING AVERAGE, NOT ON BEING GREAT.

People become conditioned to the thought that they can play the game, but they can't be star players. They may believe they can enter and participate in the race, but they cannot win it. They have learned to focus on being average, not on being great.

Here is the good news. *You can beat self-defeat.*

Count every successful step that you've made, and build upon those thoughts. Observe things that didn't go so well and make changes—this is called *progress.*

The most important things to do: don't add up setbacks, and count only your successes!

PEP TALK

Many people find that with more reading, listening, watching, and learning, they realize that they don't know as much as they thought they did. If you agree, even slightly, apply that concept to your experiences. The more you try, the more you risk, the more you experiment, the more you may experience failures and disappointment.

Does this mean that you should stop trying, stop learning, or settle for less? Absolutely not, coming to this realization is exactly the point I am making. People in this circumstance know more than they did before, they have learned that there is value from pushing on, even in the face of failure. They know what won't work or how to reach their objectives from a different path. They are learning to pivot.

Negativity and self-limiting beliefs will not create a better future. I believe you have two choices.

The first choice is to look at things negatively and decide you are less; you weren't cut out for this, and you shouldn't have tried. Later you'll tell people you are the victim, you'll carry victim values with you, and every time something doesn't work, you'll decide, once again, you are not worthy. You are, after all, the victim.

The second choice is to seek the positive: evaluate what didn't work without dwelling on the negative. Adjust, make changes, know that your success will be created only if you take chances, explore risks, and believe. Recognize you are smart because you have learned. You don't know everything, but you'll figure it out. You have heart, you have passion, and you will create your success.

People who make the second choice approach the metaphorical stairs one step at a time. They may stagger, stumble, or even fall, but their eyes remain focused on the top. They continue to climb, and when they are three steps away from achieving the final stair, they jump to the top. Worthy and self-confident, they look for the next set of stairs.

I like the second choice.

SELF-DOUBT

Have you ever wondered why some people make it big, and others seemingly try hard but never succeed? Many people quickly attribute this to luck, family money, or friends in the business. All three of those may have something to do with their success, but that isn't what makes them different.

Here is what is interesting: People who are successful and people who are not successful have something in common. They all have self-doubt. The difference is that successful people assess their self-doubt and come to the conclusion that they are better, they have positive dreams, and they continue to build self-confidence instead of doubt because they believe.

What is even more interesting?

Everything people accomplish is limited, or not, by what they believe.

TALENT

Talent. Everyone has it, and some people will use everything they've got to become the best that they can be. If it is hard, it's worth doing. If your livelihood and future depend upon it, then you must succeed. You have dedication, hard work, and a never-give-up attitude—persistence is critical for success.

Did I just describe you? If yes, you are among an elite group. Your status is likely defined by comparisons to others in your network: people you work with, friends, family, and even others in your neighborhood. Congratulations, you stand out!

So, you have talent. Remember that everyone does. How you use your talent will make the difference to your future. If you allow others to set limits for you, define you, or pass unfair judgment upon you, then you will never become all that you can be.

THEY WILL BE ENVIOUS, JEALOUS, AND RESENT YOUR SUCCESS.

Here is the bad news: people often judge, and, in the case of success, some judge others negatively. You'll know when you are creating success because someone, maybe several someones, in your network will decide they have a problem with you. They are not proud to know you, but they are happy to try to bring you down, limit your success, or tell others how or why you are not worthy. They will be envious, jealous, and resent your success. It isn't so much that they hate you; it is more likely that they hate themselves. You didn't create their lack of success. They did.

Keep this in mind: Being liked is important, but being likable is more important. Being loved by the people who really matter—that is most important. The people who love you will celebrate your success, because they admire you. Why? Because you've got talent.

WELL-DEFINED

Our experiences and perceptions help us form images. When we want to know more, we ask for the definition. Good or bad, we decide when we have the appropriate picture.

When asked about our best customer service experiences, we think carefully, sometimes not knowing what to describe. When asked about our worst experiences, images more quickly come to mind. Anger and dislike are remembered more rapidly when thinking of more recent experiences, yet longer term we often more readily recall enjoyment and happiness. Some say we try to forget unpleasant memories. The assumption is we don't want to relive past negative experiences.

Why is this important?

People form images of themselves, defined by past experiences, feedback from others, and current perceptions. We sometimes dwell too much on past experiences that we would describe as negative. We associate and, worse yet, condition our future based on past images of ourselves, especially negative ones, sadly.

If you are replaying past negative experiences over and over again in your mind—stop. Forget about the time you didn't measure up, the time someone suggested you didn't have the talent, or the time someone made you feel like less. Your past isn't what defines you. It is your future that will define you. Past struggles, hurdles, and obstacles have prepared you to be ready for bigger challenges. You are not inadequate, untalented, or otherwise finished. Think of an image of who you want to be, and make it a good one.

Define yourself. Define yourself well!

POSSIBLE

People may have told you it wasn't possible. You're different. The difference for you isn't about doubt, fear, or self-limiting beliefs—that is the difference for them. The difference for you is about desire, confidence, and action.

Desire may be intrinsic motivation, but I believe intrinsic motivation comes to life through inspiration. You see something, feel something, and admire something so much it inspires you to take your own course of action. It may be to help, please, or contribute to someone else's effort, or it may be a personal desire you want to achieve. People model behaviors constantly. Like it or not, our actions or inactions provide role models for someone else.

However, confidence isn't about duplicating, mimicking, or plagiarizing. Why? Because you can't fake confidence. It is something that doesn't sell from fake. You've heard the mantra, "Fake it until you make it," but that really doesn't hold true in a personal quest for more. It may be true when getting through a difficult situation or circumstance, but it will never propel you to the growth that you need.

If you have the desire and the confidence, your final ingredient is action. Action will make the difference. Procrastination, hesitation, and fear will never allow you to achieve all that is possible. It's strange what excuses your mind makes. The timing isn't right, the situation is not perfect, and you don't have the money or resources to pursue it right now. Any or all of those circumstances may be true, or they may just be excuses driven by fear, causing hesitation, and resulting in procrastination.

Your goals have to pass the reasonability test, but all things within reason are possible. If someone is telling you that it isn't possible, that person doesn't know you.

CHAPTER SUMMARY

Confidence may exist more in our minds than in our hearts. Our hearts are filled with desire and passion, but our minds tend to either stop action or accelerate it. The greatest thing about confidence is that it can be developed, but it takes a strong mind to develop it.

Typically we don't ignore negative feedback. We try really hard, but when we get negative feedback it hurts, causes anger, and perhaps makes us fearful about our next move. That is everything that confidence is not and perhaps it is why it is so easy for us to get off track.

Many people have more wins than they realize. They just don't focus on wins. Instead they focus on the memory of hurt, anger, and frustration. If you have passed a test, completed high school, obtained a job, gotten a drivers' license, made a dollar, saved a dollar, spent a dollar, risked something, lost something, found something—do you see a pattern here? We've all done something; we have reason to celebrate our success, not drown in the agony of ridicule, negative labels, or failures.

Build more confidence. Focus on your best performances, your successes, and your true friends, family, and those who love and support you. Confidence is yours to build or to lose, but you only lose it if you allow yourself to. You've probably heard or said the expression "gain confidence." It is a truth. Confidence is gained by what you focus on. It is more in your mind than in your heart.

Dennis E. Gilbert

CHAPTER 6

FOCUS

One reason so few of us achieve what we truly want is that we never direct our focus; we never concentrate our power. Most people dabble their way through life, never deciding to master anything in particular.

Tony Robbins[1]

Lessons on focus are often hard to learn. Part of the reason is that our subconscious minds tell us that throwing our energy and effort at many things must result in something. Unfortunately the reality of that logic will not guarantee any results. In fact, a lack of focus can create a lack of success in everything that you try. Too many people and businesses fall victim to this approach.

I like to call it the spray and pray approach. You spray your marketplace or environment with tons of service offerings, solutions, or products; then you pray that something happens. As a result, you are not effective in any. It feels risky to narrow your focus, but your results may be better than expected.

Spray and pray may work in the farmer's field, it may work with an air freshener and your cat box, but it often produces less-than-favorable results as a personal or business strategy. This is another reason why confidence is so important. Confident people and businesses tend to have a presence that creates results, sometimes seemingly without trying.

Do you try to have or be every solution, or do you master a select few or just one solution? You won't find happiness by being the one others want you to be. You'll find happiness by creating the person you know you can be. The best part about knowing who you want to be is not the realization that you have to push hard for your goals. The best part is having the knowledge and understanding that you are not wasting any time trying to become the person someone else wants you to be.

What costs more: the price of success, the price of failure, or the price of staying the same? Many may say it depends. I believe if you depend on doing the same old thing, you may come to realize that doing what feels safe or comes easily has the most expensive price of all.

LIVING MOMENTS

Successful people take a deep breath and reflect on their accomplishments. They find both pride and tranquility as they consider their family, their home, their job, their career, or their business. Successful people savor the moment; they keep it as not only a positive reflection, but also as a building block for their future.

Creating success is creating happiness. By definition it may be different for everyone. Successful people have a focus; their focus is on the positive. This focus does not include reliving negative and painful experiences from the past; it comes from the vision and image of their success.

We learn from mistakes and failures, but successful people do not dwell on them. They take away the learning and turn it into productive growth. They recognize that doing the same thing over and over again but expecting different results is not the answer. They adapt, change, and take responsible risks.

I believe that your ability to create your success requires you to draw on the energy and excitement of successful moments of the past. It does not require reliving painful, hurtful, or embarrassing shortcomings.

Imagine what is possible. Live your moments!

ON THE GROUND

Only you can create your next big break. Many people often believe that those who are more successful have never experienced any tragedy, hard times, or self-doubt when in fact these people have probably experienced more challenges than others realize. The difference is that when they are down they pick themselves back up, they don't wait for someone else to do it, and *they* do it.

You may be thinking, "I already know this; it is old news."

If you think it is old news, ask yourself if you've accomplished your goals. If not, I have some news for you. Unlike sports teams, most people don't realize they are down until late in the game. If you're not on the road to your next goal, or you can't see the finish line, it may mean that you're on the ground.

Pick yourself up—no one else is going to do it.

HAPPY WITH UNHAPPY

Some people are happy with unhappy, or so it seems. Unless you are a therapist you probably shouldn't focus too much of your energy on trying to fix unhappy people. Of course caring for close friends or loved ones is very important, but sacrificing your emotional health in an effort to try to fix them is probably not a good idea.

OFTEN, THEY DO NOTHING, GIVE LITTLE OR NO EFFORT, AND THEN BLAME OTHERS FOR THEIR SHORTCOMINGS.

Changing other people is very difficult, and probably impossible if they really don't want to change. Unfortunately some people seek the easy road. Often, they do nothing, give little or no effort, and then blame others for their shortcomings.

Here is what I believe: You can't afford to "own" someone else's problem. You can provide suggestions, guidance, and recommendations, but then it is up to them to take the initiative and work hard for change. It is their responsibility to reach for more, be disciplined, and take action. If they choose not to do that, it is their issue, not yours.

This is not about being selfish, it is about being balanced. It seems that most people believe success is happiness—that is, unless you are happy with being unhappy.

OVERWHELMED

Too much to do and too little time, too many problems to solve and the rate of new problems seems to exceed the rate of solved problems. Becoming overwhelmed is the start of a downward ride—a ride no one wants to take.

Overwhelmed feelings make you feel out of control. Those feelings block you from forward motion and inhibit you from creating your success. Feeling overwhelmed tends to sneak up on people. One day you're doing great, then suddenly you are overwhelmed. People who successfully manage these feelings have at least three things in common:

1. They transition through change quickly.

2. They are highly efficient at prioritizing.

3. They expect the unexpected.

Improving your skills in managing your personal or professional life doesn't necessarily require a specific talent, but it does require your attention and a meaningful effort to create balance. Your ability to prioritize, transition through change, and expect the unexpected is much greater when looking forward through the windshield instead of into the rearview mirror. Remember to keep accelerating away from what is in the rearview mirror, focused on what you see in front of you, not fixed on what you've left behind.

This is your ride. Make it a good one!

SHORTCUTS AND QUICK FIXES

People often look for shortcuts or quick fixes. Your future success probably will not come to fruition through either of these. That is the bad news.

Here is the good news: having an appropriate focus can help you achieve the next step on your path. You can develop a better focus through three simple steps:

1. What has been successful for you up to this point? Do more of that!

2. What haven't you tried because it feels too risky? Explore more of that!

3. Use these two questions to hone your focus and stay the course. Persistence is key.

Typically there are no shortcuts or quick fixes. Persistence will get you through the next step and beyond.

PERSISTENCE IS SMART

Persistence is different.

Persistence is having a consistent goal and expecting to change your strategy and tactics as necessary to get results. Persistence is not doing the same thing over and over. It is not the status quo. It means you won't just do things differently, you'll do different things.

Persistence is change.

Many people struggle by playing it safe when it comes to change. Consciously or subconsciously, some people talk themselves into what they believe is safe. They compromise on their goals, justify why they can't do something, or wait to see what happens for others. However, this kind of thinking will get you nowhere. Instead live for change, change to live, or try to catch up, but if you're trying to catch up you're probably already too late.

Persistence is focus, not safety or risk.

In a world of constant change, playing it safe may be too risky. Safe may feel smart, until someone else gets the sale, exceeds your performance, or steals your promotion. On the other hand, playing it safe does have its advantages; you won't have to worry about paying more taxes, going on your dream vacation, or trying to decide which new car to buy.

People don't achieve big results when they play it (totally) safe. Safety and risk should be evaluated; but a lack of focus, having the wrong focus, or no focus at all has much more to do with why some people come up short.

Simply put, persistence is smart.

FOCUSED

The word *focus* means to make something fuzzy become clear, or to concentrate or apply energy and effort more narrowly as compared to broadly. There are a variety of ways to define focus. When it comes to achieving your goals, perhaps nothing is more important.

Some believe their chances of success are much greater when they spread out resources and go after many opportunities, as compared to focusing only on a special few. There appears to be the logic that more chances are better. Perhaps it is true with a lottery, but when it comes to your life, career, or the success of your team, probably not so much. More chances are not directly proportional to more results.

Resources are required for our pursuit of goals and success. Since our resources are finite, we have to find ways to make the best use of them. Time, money, and people are all resources with limitations. If you spend these pursuing many opportunities instead of pursuing just one or a limited few, it is likely your results will be fewer rather than more.

Consider these examples: You can spend a little time, but not enough, on fifty things, or spend focused time on two or three. You can spend a few dollars of your marketing budget on each of thirty-five activities, or spend more of the same total budget on a few focused channels. You can assign twelve people to pursue twelve totally different things or have groups of four focus on three specific things.

You can use your resources without focus, or you can focus on effective use of your resources, but you'll never do both.

You may find that being focused on nothing will get you nothing.

CHAPTER SUMMARY

Sometimes it is the simple things, things that seem to defy logic that were once considered from a different approach or angle suddenly make the most sense. Focus may be one of those simple things.

Logically the more attempts we make, the greater our chances of success, but if those attempts are very scattered this becomes false. The picture becomes clearer when we are more focused, and our chances for success increase, not decrease.

There is a level of intensity associated with focus: the more intense, persistent, and committed you are, the more likely you will enjoy a positive outcome. It's not about more chances, it is about the same chances being narrowly framed and precise. If you only had one chance, one shot, just one opportunity—how would you use it?

Your career, happiness, life—cumulatively you have just one shot. Does it make sense to focus?

Yes!

CHAPTER 7

RAINMAKERS

I don't believe in pessimism. If something doesn't come up the way you want, forge ahead. If you think it's going to rain, it will.

Clint Eastwood[1]

There really isn't anything mystical about rainmakers: they make it rain. People in business who get the sales flowing, orders coming in, or customers engaged are rainmakers. When you need something to happen, they can pull it off. It may be a one-person show, or it could be the sales leaders, marketing and advertising experts, or even the CEO. Rainmakers make it rain.

Does it take someone talented, gifted, or really special? Let's answer that by saying it takes someone who is confident, committed, and results oriented. Do they need some talent? Sure, they need some talent. Do they need a special gift or to be really special? Depending on how you look at it, no, they don't.

What allows rainmakers to make it rain? Their mind-sets are completely different. They are not focused on the way it has been—they are focused on the way it will be. If you listen closely, many people will tell you they are waiting for their next big break. Being positive and having a positive outlook is good, but dreaming of big, audacious goals is what propels some to excel. Remember that action is often what separates dreamers from achievers. If you find yourself waiting as opposed to taking action, you may find yourself waiting for a long, long time.

Big breaks happen, but they happen to people who take action. Unfortunately, many people are preprogrammed to take a backseat and do only the minimum required to get by. All the while, they claim they are one step away from the next breakthrough. Yet they wait, perhaps for a break that will never come. They need to break away; they need to break their own subconscious rules. Subconsciously we often set limits.

If you want to make it rain, you need to believe in audacious goals and set no limits.

RAINMAKERS DON'T JUST MAKE THINGS DAMP—THEY MAKE IT POUR.

It seems everyone wants or needs a little rain from time to time. In business, we cherish people who can make it rain, especially after a long dry spell. In our personal or individual development, the same is true. Sometimes we just need it to rain. The messages in this chapter can be the rain clouds for your success, but you still have to make it rain. Rainmakers don't just make things damp—they make it pour. Sprinkling a little of your effort all over the place isn't rain. It will require a whole lot more to turn an ordinary sprinkle into the downpour you've been waiting for.

WHAT CROWD?

The bad news: Some people blame others for their lack of success. They believe that they don't get enough good breaks, they are chronically unlucky, or someone else cheated to achieve what they desire.

The good news: you don't have to be one of the numbers statistically represented in the "bad news" crowd. Of course there are people who are more fortunate; some people win the lottery or inherit financial wealth from relatives. Remember, you have the ability to choose your success, and it is certainly not always about financial wealth. You can take the risks, make the sacrifices, and reap the rewards. You can enjoy your success!

Which crowd are you in?

STRIKE A MATCH

People often ask me about team building or teamwork training. Businesses strive to get the most from their employees, which is a smart plan. Many of us have heard or even said the idiom "fire in your belly," and we know this means using passion and energy to fight for something that we strongly believe in.

Work groups and teams who "set themselves on fire" pursue something they are passionate about. They become engaged and fueled in a seemingly unstoppable way. They are unflappable under pressure, and they may become more intense when the stakes are higher. Successful people have experienced this, successful businesses know this, and successful teams do this.

As you approach your work at your next team meeting or during your next strategy session, you should think, "Strike a match. Let's do this!"

GO IN EARLY

This isn't one of those "early bird gets the worm" stories, or about arriving at work before your start time. Although both of those scenarios may be a good idea, this is about improving your results, increasing your chances for success, and knowing when the timing is right.

When presented with change, many people hesitate. They are unsure of what to expect, they are not convinced it is a good idea, and many of them have experienced failure to change in the past. All of this leaves them more hesitant instead of energized. This is where people get the timing all wrong. Early adopters have a much greater chance of success as compared to those who come in later in the life cycle. Remember the dot-com boom and bust? Early adopters made a fortune, while late adopters didn't make out so well. Being first or early in the cycle of any idea, product, or service positions you to achieve better results.

The reason for this is simple: everything has a life cycle that we often see graphically depicted as a bell curve. In the beginning, the line heads up the chart. As time goes on the line climbs higher and higher, until at one point it peaks. Then the benefits that made it go up the chart start to be less recognized or valued, and the line starts to go down. Late adopters come in when the benefits are diminishing, limiting their chances for success. They missed all the energy, excitement, and momentum the early adopters used as their strategic advantage. We see these cycles everywhere, from technology to advertising to social media.

People search for the right timing, the next big idea, or something that will change their futures. Often they wonder how they missed their window. Opportunities happen frequently. The problem is they may be disguised as change, put off through hesitation, or avoided out of fear.

Early adopters achieve more. Go in early.

EXCUSES, EXCUSES

That is a great excuse!

Have you ever heard, said, or thought that?

Excuses often develop as a result of self-doubt. Sadly, when we face obstacles or challenges, we may quickly remember the time we came up short, let someone down, or failed to please someone with our performance. As a result we may develop the belief that we don't have the talent, qualifications, or money to pursue the next step. Of course, sometimes this is true, but in other cases this is just an excuse.

Whether you label it self-protection, action anxiety, or a form of fear, people make excuses. While there are lots of problems with excuses, probably the biggest is that they simply stop you from taking any action at all. In most cases your success is not a spectator sport, so lack of action means lack of results.

Let's face it, excuses are useless. Hesitation will not position you for success. Neither will being frozen with fear. Your success, or lack of it, is conditioned by action.

Change your outcomes by turning self-doubt into no-doubt. Take action!

PAYING FOR CHEESE

Everyone looks for free stuff. We are often prompted by free products, free samples, and free services. This is only the beginning; the list is long. There is an old saying: "The only free cheese is in the mousetrap." Some believe this "baiting" tactic will one day implode in a swirl of negative consumer behavior.

When it comes to your life and career, I believe nothing is free. Sure, you may be able to get some free advice or some free reading material, but you most likely will not experience the kind of future you're hoping for if you expect to achieve your goals without paying.

The price is relative, but it certainly isn't free. You pay in effort, sacrifice, and discipline in order to achieve the things that are really worth something to you. If you're searching for "free cheese," good luck. You're likely not going to get more by doing less. People who do more typically do more by choice.

Expect to pay for your "cheese."

PART OF SOMETHING

Like some animals, man finds comfort in teams, packs, and herds. This behavior, which many believe is part of a natural process that comes to us through evolution, is often viewed as strength. At the same time it is restrictive, because it often supports little movement against the norms of the group.

Many business leaders will quickly tell you that they are in full support of creative thinking and it is an inherent part of their culture. Yet they often impose strict belief systems throughout their business that suggest never straying from protocol or design standards. This is a mind-set that steers people (employees) away from being creative innovators.

FEAR OF REMOVAL, OTHERWISE KNOWN AS THE FEAR OF SEPARATION, MAY KEEP A TEAM INTACT AT THE EXPENSE OF CREATIVE THINKING THAT GENERATES FUTURE OPTIONS.

It seems that the goal should be high quality with minimal waste while also allowing flexibility for innovation. This makes sense, yet performance standards are seldom measured for innovation. In fact, trying something out of the norm may be viewed as strictly forbidden and could result in your being removed from the team. Fear of removal, otherwise known as the fear of separation, may keep a team intact at the expense of creative thinking that generates future options.

While this may be true within businesses, it may also become true for individuals hoping to achieve new breakthroughs. If we are programmed to group norms, perhaps we set limitations on new or creative thinking as a barrier for creating options. At a minimum it may limit our desire to risk, and in more extreme cases it has become a restrictive form of self-defeat.

You have a choice and I believe that:

- Doing what everyone else does is a movement; you're part of the crowd.

- Doing what no one else does starts a movement; you're part of an option.

You do have a choice—right?

CHAPTER SUMMARY

Rainmakers face choices too. Limited observations perhaps draw the conclusion that luck just happens for rainmakers, as if they are the chosen ones and some mystical aura surrounds them. Not so much. Rainmakers make it rain because they are focused more positively, and they position themselves for more positive action.

People are drawn to energy and excitement. There isn't really much excitement associated with missed opportunities, coming up short on sales goals, or filing for bankruptcy. These are negative energies, the kind of feeling that most people push hard to avoid. In contrast, people who are happy see new opportunities, believe they can achieve more, and are confident. They tend to inspire that same spirit within others. Their outlook is different.

Consider yourself engaged in a discussion with some very successful people. They mention some struggles—times when they thought they couldn't make it, and how they walked ten miles to school and it was uphill both ways. Yet as you engage in conversation with them, they are happy, excited, and successful. Somehow that inspires you and motivates you to consider how you can reach for more.

Now imagine yourself on a park bench, pigeons pecking around your feet for food. A man sits down next to you. He is dressed in worn-out shoes and ragged clothes. There are indications that he hasn't had a bath or a shave for longer than you care to imagine. You try to engage in conversation, but he is tired, weak, and shows little or no energy to talk. Suddenly you feel his pain; perhaps your heart aches for this man, and you wonder how his life evolved to this point where he sits on this bench in such poor condition.

While these situations sharply contrast with each other, we often become what surrounds us. Grief, sorrow, and dead-end roads leave us unmotivated, disengaged, and victimized. Happiness, success, and energy excite and motivate us to do more. These are rainmakers: they see things differently, they surround themselves with positives, they view only the positives, and they quickly jump past obstacles because they never consider defeat.

Are they special? Their minds are programmed differently, and because of this they get different results. They personally reinforce a "can do" attitude as opposed to thinking, "Why even try?" Their presence is uplifting, not downshifting; people are drawn toward them, not repelled by them.

They are rainmakers; they make it rain.

CHAPTER 8

LEADERSHIP

If you think you can do a thing or think you can't do a thing, you're right.

Henry Ford[1]

An observation I've made after many years spent in leadership roles, combined with years as an organization development consultant and coach, is that the most significant thing holding people back is their mind-set. Many would argue that it is luck, opportunity, or money. All of those are good excuses, but not reasons.

Mind-set really cannot be faked. We've all heard the idiom "fake it until you make it." In some circles that may elevate you to the next hurdle you need to jump, but in the long term you can't fake it. Some will argue that they have faked it for some time, but in reality, if they are addressing their level of competence or confidence, they likely have more muscle than they realize.

Our words, body language, and confidence are all different when we fake it. In leadership roles, try faking it to make it, and people will not believe it. It's too evident.

People sometimes debate leadership roles and strategy. Some claim that you should lead from the front; others claim that the front is a good choice, but you can also lead from the back. Still others claim that leadership is completely situational, and how you lead depends on the team, the situation, and the challenge. Lead long enough and you will likely find that your leadership style, if effective, is at some level situational.

That is what makes great leaders great. They have the ability to lead during varying adverse conditions. With that said, they also have to be able to lead during good times, not just under duress—or do they? Public and private corporations often seek top-level talent that supports the business's current market conditions, financial status, and strategy. The belief is that the right talent is situational.

Another common misconception is that each business only has one leader, or that leadership is reserved for just a few precious positions at or near the top of the organizational chart. Great leadership is needed everywhere in the business, including in those who lead committees, teams, and culture, and sometimes even in those who help guide the thinking and decisions of those at the top.

If you have spent any time in the work force, you undoubtedly will also recognize that sometimes there are people in high-ranking positions who are lousy leaders. You will also, of course, recognize the opposite: sometimes there are people with little or no formal authority who possess extraordinary leadership talent. This might highlight the question of whether leaders can be made. Are they simply born into existence?

There are lots of theories about leaders, followers, and teams. One theory is that leadership is about people (followers) developing a belief in the leader. The thought is, "Join me, or you'll never go anywhere." I don't subscribe to that theory. I believe leadership is less about developing belief in the leader and more about developing a belief in the followers. When you create values, traditions, ethics, products, services, or a brand, you've created a belief in those who choose to follow. The belief in the leader then comes naturally.

Belief is powerful—you can't fake it.

GOOD BOSS

One of the most common training needs expressed to me by small businesses is the need for leadership training and development. Businesses that employ fifty or five hundred or even more employees often find themselves scrambling to develop their formal leaders. Many of these businesses have become successful largely by promoting from within, a commendable and well-supported tactic.

THEY ARE EXCELLENT TECHNICALLY, BUT NOT IN POSITIONS WHERE THEY MUST MANAGE PEOPLE.

The bad part of this is that often the employees who are promoted to supervisors, managers, or directors were the stars of their departments or work groups. This is bad news because often these people are experts in their fields, but lack the knowledge and expertise to be effective leaders. They are excellent technically, but not in positions where they must manage people.

Here is the good news. Many of these hard-charging heroes who made their way up the corporate ladder absolutely have the foundational skills to build and grow into their new positions. Training in the areas of effective communication, emotional intelligence, and critical thinking are all good starters when positioning them for new (up-the-ladder) job roles.

Are you a good leader? Is your boss a good leader?

BUDDY SYSTEM

The buddy system in the workplace may mean different things to different people. Some view the buddy system as a teamwork effort, and therefore a good thing—something where people are helping people. Others view the buddy system as a ticket to become a fast-tracker, a one-way ticket based on friendship or "political" support that will get them closer to the top faster than any other method.

Teamwork and people helping people, with a focus on creating outstanding products or services, is a great thing. Helping someone in need in the workplace, someone who appropriately "has your back," can be a great thing. A clique of "buddies" who stand together creating personal and professional opportunities only for like-minded people in their clique may not be such a good thing.

Do you know of a buddy system? How does it work?

COMMUNICATION COSTS

Business and interpersonal communication are changing. Communication etiquette is entering a new age, but should it? If you work in a business environment where communication is important—and I would like to ask when isn't it?—this is for you.

I believe in an ethical code of conduct that includes instructions on how to be a good communicator. Here is a tip for everyone who uses e-mail as a communication vehicle: be courteous, be kind, and do what you expect of others.

When the subject of e-mail communication arises in my workshops, it usually includes two areas of concern: (1) junk mail, and (2) no return or no response to a sent e-mail. Nobody wants to be overloaded, so think twice about what you send. Do the recipients really need this information? On the flip side, when someone takes the time to send you a direct e-mail (not spam), be professionally courteous and give them a timely response.

Some people believe in leaving nothing to chance. Avoidance, delays, and not responding gives permission to those whom you communicate with to make assumptions, develop their own answers, and share those thoughts with others.

Communication costs—what can you afford?

ACCOUNTABILITY BREAKDOWN

It isn't so much that accountability causes a breakdown as the commitment of delivering to others does. Many people tell me, "Hey, I'm busy too. I have my own action items to worry about." I often encounter teams struggling with accountability, whether it involves managers, peer-to-peer groups, or direct reports.

The Problem

The problem is that much of this has to do with organizational culture and past common practice. If deadlines are excusable, then few will take them seriously. Direct reports—those within businesses who represent the employee population at large or those who report to a boss, as compared to those who are bosses—may have complaints about micromanagement, which causes many supervisors to just dump and run. Peer-to-peer accountability often convinces workers that the commitment is more about the individual and less about the business. Ultimately they prefer to work on their own tasks, seldom worrying about another person's to-do list.

The Solution

Based on my experiences, I see three things that will help improve workplace accountability:

1. Do not micromanage, but do set expectations with a report-in or check-in time.

2. Focus on why this task or information is important to the team or business, not on why it is important to the individual.

3. Set positive examples and highlight occurrences where commitment paid off. Avoid negative references, such as what may happen if it isn't completed.

Peer-to-peer accountability is often the most challenging, since people may be programmed to only respond when the boss jumps in. Avoid creating a culture of run-and-tell to get things done—it discourages teamwork and wastes everyone's time.

CULTURE OF BELIEF

Belief is important, commitment to your belief is more important, and if you work with a team it should become a shared belief—a culture of belief. Buy-in is a word or phrase that probably belongs on the buzzword bingo card. Many business managers and executives talk about buy-in. They recognize the need to create it, and talk about achieving it, but do they actually succeed?

WHEN YOU GIVE POSITIVE REINFORCEMENT AND ENCOURAGEMENT TO OTHERS, IT HELPS BUILD THEIR SELF-CONFIDENCE, IMPROVES MORALE, AND CREATES BUY-IN.

If you are trying to create buy-in, then creating a culture of belief starts with you. You have to believe in the cause, or be so compelling in your actions and behaviors that you create a perception of belief. (I suggest that you believe. If you don't, then why are you trying to convince others?) When you give positive reinforcement and encouragement to others, it helps build their self-confidence, improves morale, and creates buy-in.

Take action, get involved, and show role-model behaviors and actions that support the cause. Most of all, reinforce others' beliefs by recognizing and congratulating them on actions or efforts that are consistent with what you are trying to achieve. Teams energized with belief in the cause will outperform others, exceed goals, and reach for more.

Create a culture of belief.

Do you believe in them?

FRIENDS OF SUCCESS

What limits your success?

There may be many limiting factors, but one of the least understood or recognized is the idea that our social environment may condition the amount of success we discover.

Friends sometimes:

- don't like being outperformed.

- are envious or jealous.

- want to keep you down or hold you back.

These friends are not friends of success; they are friends who (sadly) help us limit our ability to achieve more. We frame our goals, our passions, and our success. We frame them based on self-esteem and self-efficacy, sometimes we frame them based on bench-mark data, past performance data, or even perceived management expectations. Operating within our frames allows us to either continue to grow and reach for more, or keeps us boxed in and limits what we believe we can achieve.

Friends of success help us discover our next steps. They help us make positive and productive changes. They help us create and fulfill dreams—dreams of our future.

PEOPLE KNOW

Business leaders may often proclaim: "We've been talking about this and talking about this. I don't understand why these people don't get it."

People attend meetings, have business lunches and dinners, and go on trips together. They talk and talk and talk about problems and concerns. They formulate strategies and take action.

Sometimes they forget to share the message. They have discussed it so much and it is so fluent on their minds that they assume everyone knows.

I work with a lot of businesses that struggle with communication problems. In fact, most businesses probably have room to improve. This seemingly simple task of information-sharing is one of the biggest issues causing miscommunication. This happens easily as management teams relentlessly discuss what to do and how to do it; they sometimes falsely assume that everyone knows.

People know.

Don't they?

CHAPTER SUMMARY

The concept of leadership may be underused, overused, partially used, intentionally used, and sometimes abused. A great amount of work, theory, and research has been performed relating to the topic of leadership. There are books about great leaders, bad leaders, well-known leaders, and little-known leaders. I believe leadership is much more about a focus on the followers than it is about the leaders.

You seldom see a business book or research work related to followers. Sometimes you do, of course, but the topic is far less popular than those associated with the pride and egos of those we call leaders.

We confuse leadership with management and management with supervisors—or do we? Are they synonymous? Sometimes yes and sometimes no.

The training and speaking side of my business is often about developing leaders. Some of these people have direct reports and some do not. Some have titles that include supervisor, manager, director, and vice president, and some do not have titles. Some are great, some are not, and some simply don't care. Are they all leaders?

I think not.

Leadership is about responsibility, critical thinking, action, and progress. Leaders can lead and inspire, although in the workplace they may not have direct reports. The leader today may not be the appropriate leader for tomorrow—unless they are successful at pivoting.

Leaders build networks, tribes, and culture. They know when to act, when to listen, when to pull from the front and when to push from the back. They are courageous, determined, and persistent. People follow them because they are inspiring, trustworthy, selfless, and confident.

We need more leaders.

CHAPTER 9

PERSISTENCE

To make our way, we must have firm resolve, persistence, tenacity. We must gear ourselves to work hard all the way. We can never let up.

Ralph Bunche[1]

Talent can be beaten, but it is hard to overcome heart.

Persistence is a passion for me. I learned as a teenager that persistence pays off. Lessons from so many years ago still ring true for me. I often meet people with tremendous talent. They make their area of expertise or technical ability look like child's play. Sadly, many of them never achieve. Sometimes it seems like things that come easily to us are the things we find to be boring or a waste of time. Bored people often don't make the most of their talent. Challenge stimulates us.

People, teams, and businesses are beaten every day, not because they lack talent but perhaps because they lack heart. Unless everything you do gets results beyond your wildest dreams, you must consider the idea that persistence is not doing the same thing over and over again; *that* we could define as insanity. Persistence is about having consistent goals and an undying focus over and over again. Persistence may require us to change our approach, but not the desired outcomes or goals.

People and businesses with heart are difficult to beat. With heart they have the ability to learn new skills, techniques, and knowledge; when equipped with tools, their hearts overcome those with talent who lack hearts. If you are sleeping, they will beat you. Chances are if your talent allows progress with limited effort, you often feel no challenge, and boredom allows you to let your guard down. People with heart will eat your lunch, first while you are sleeping and later while you watch.

Persistence is not overbearing. Persistence does not imply wearing out your welcome. Persistence is what takes you from your vision through your mission to accomplish goals. It is a fluid process regarding everything but your desire to achieve. It is not about too many telephone calls, too many e-mail messages, or too many uninvited visits; that could be labeled as harassment. Persistence is a focused and undying pursuit. It doesn't collapse under pressure; it doesn't take holidays—it is persistent.

Certainly, persistent people and businesses also strike an appropriate balance of push and pull, work and play, audacity and timidity. Outside of persistence, perhaps nothing is more important than balance; without balance, nothing will persevere long-term. Balance is a critical factor for persistent pursuit.

Dare to dream. Dare to have audacious goals, and have persistent focus in achieving them. Keep in mind that thinking about what you want over and over again is dreaming, while action over and over again is focus. So give it up today. Take a risk on trying something new or a little bit different, and you'll have success or failure. Play it safe and nothing changes. What is most important to remember is that failure is not the opposite of success—failure is staying stuck.

PERSISTENCE AND DREAMS

Do you know a person who complains about a lack of success? Do you know people who feel down, disengaged, and resentful about their position in life or their career?

Their success starts with a dream. Their dream needs to become their passion. Most of all, they must first believe in themselves and then in their dream. They need to be persistent and view their dream as an ongoing process with specific goals. If they don't have specific goals, they will never achieve them.

ASK THEM ABOUT THEIR DREAMS AND THEY CANNOT DESCRIBE ONE, OR THE CONVERSATION CHANGES TO WOULD HAVE, COULD HAVE, SHOULD HAVE— AND THEN SHIFTS TO BLAME.

The success of others feels criminal to those who believe they missed out, were looked over, or just not lucky. Ask them about their dreams and they cannot describe one, or the conversation changes to would have, could have, should have—and then shifts to blame.

The only crimes here are that the decisions and choices that they made, or didn't make, are directly proportionate to their success.

Start with a dream. Finish with success.

PERSONAL ENERGY—TWO CHOICES

There are times when you feel like you get so much accomplished, and times when you feel like you accomplished nothing. We often encounter people who have accomplished a lot, and people who have accomplished very little. I've noticed something about people: the difference in success comes from how they use their energy.

I believe that you have two choices. One choice is to evaluate what you are doing, both short- and long-term, and consistently monitor your progress. Similar to time management, project management, or even business management, you have to evaluate the timelines and milestones and be sure you are using your energy wisely and staying focused on positive outcomes.

A second choice is to haphazardly roll through life. You don't have any real plan, you don't recognize missed opportunities, and most likely you have no set timelines—no milestones—and so you have absolutely nothing with which to monitor your progress. You use your energy to talk about what could have or should have been, but because you typically accomplish very little, you have no foundation to build confidence and to learn to make better choices.

Here is something else I've noticed about people: choice one people are probably reading this, while choice two people are probably wondering why they should.

DUSTY MIRROR

Do you self-assess? Do you take the time and opportunity to consider where you are currently, where you are going, how you measure up, and if you are on track? If you don't or haven't done it lately, you should.

One of the biggest factors that may condition your success is what you see when you look in the mirror. Once in a while, I meet people who feel down on their luck. Perhaps they are struggling in their personal lives or their jobs, or they are business owners who feel like they have tried everything but nothing is working out the way they wanted.

One thing I learned is that we can do a lot with hopes and dreams. People who are committed to making their cause a success will work tirelessly as they pursue and create their future. Successful people are persistent.

IF WHAT YOU TRIED ISN'T WORKING, TRY SOMETHING NEW.

Has it been some time since you really stopped to reflect and self-assess? Can you see yourself? or has dust accumulated on your mirror? If it's dusty, wipe off that dust and look for what is great, fabulous, and inspiring about you, your job, or your business. If what you tried isn't working, try something new. If you have tried many things, what was more successful when compared with the others?

Is your mirror dusty? Personally, I think you've got this; go get some results!

MACHINES

Whether their work is easy or hard, successful people find ways to move forward; they are persistent.

Some people break down and fold up. Give them adverse conditions and a couple of setbacks and they throw in the towel. Too much challenge, too many uphill battles, and they quit. Others don't stop. They are like machines. Adverse conditions don't weaken or lessen their output; instead, they challenge them and spring them into action. Times of challenge are when they perform at their best.

Some machines do break down. Others continue on, and, instead of breaking down, they break records. They improve efficiencies, output, and quality. They are relentless and unstoppable. They don't really have good and bad days because they only focus on making every day the absolute best. They live for this.

Which machine are you?

NO GUARANTEE

Nothing guarantees that you will achieve what you are striving for—nothing except *persistence.*

Persistence is perhaps the single most important ingredient to help you obtain your success. One of the most common barriers to success is giving up too easily, or perhaps giving up when a breakthrough is just about to emerge. Many factors, including things like timing, the economy, and resources, may condition the pace or level of your success, but persistence is what will make the difference.

FAILURE TO REACH IS FAILURE TO SUCCEED; EVERYTHING ELSE IS A LEARNING OPPORTUNITY.

All things within reason are within your reach. Failure to reach is failure to succeed; everything else is a learning opportunity.

Create your own guarantee.

FACING REALITY

Taking risks and pushing for success sometimes results in disappointment. Disappointment, while not desirable, helps you remain focused on the end result. It gives you the opportunity to keep your path fluid and make adjustments as necessary, and reminds you of why you are so determined to achieve your success.

Facing reality is not always easy, but it is another step on the path that leads to the road that takes you to where you belong. Some believe that your destiny is predetermined; I believe that you create it. Face the reality of your circumstances, and you will discover the correct answers to the choices you need to make.

What is your reality?

BEING AVERAGE

The path to achieving your success is never easy. It is easy to deliver an average performance and obtain average results. It is easy to perform above average for a short period of time. It is easy to talk about what could have been and should have been, and cast blame or make excuses.

People who are committed to achieving their success are persistent; they deliver above-average performances day in and day out. They do whatever it takes to raise the bar on their performances. When working with a team or business, they not only raise the bar for themselves, they raise the bar for everyone.

Developing an attitude of doing whatever it takes doesn't end with improving your personal best. It creates an atmosphere of success that causes the competition to make decisions about their future. Some will give up; some will do whatever it takes.

Are you doing whatever it takes?

PERSISTENCE IS FIRE

Persistence isn't smoke, it is a controlled fire.

People often believe they are persistent, but in reality few truly are. Sure, they may be persistent about asking questions, asking for favors, or even about follow-through, but they are often not persistent about achieving their goals, exceeding their personal best, or attaining what they consider success.

Talk only goes so far, and talking about what you want to achieve persistently is not the same as pursuing it with persistence. People often stop, abort, and just give up when they face adversity. Unwanted challenges and obstacles may cause them to reflect on the words of underachievers, further halting progress through a progressive state of mind infected with underachieving, self-limiting beliefs. Sadly, the focus then becomes *I can't, I won't, and I should have never tried.*

Persistence is the act of striving in the face of adversity. Baffled onlookers, satisfied with mediocrity, watch the efforts of those who are persistent in both amazement and disbelief. There is nothing wrong with being satisfied, but then you can't be envious, jealous, and judgmental of those who achieve more through their dedicated pursuit.

Persistence is more than talk; it's more than smoke. Persistence is a burning desire. It is about passion, intensity, and tenacity.

Are you persistent?

You can be.

TENACITY REQUIRED

Is it fair to say that roughly 50 percent of those who voted in the United States of America presidential election in 2012 were disappointed in the results? The number of votes for the winning party was only slightly over 50 percent, as I recall.

This reminds me of one of the most important aspects of creating success—tenacity.

Today many Americans need to face reality. If you are focused on building your success, the election results and who is right and who is wrong are not the most important issues. Working on your plan for moving ahead is the most important issue you now face.

When I awoke the morning following the election, I feared that while half of the country would be celebrating, the other half would be considering giving up. Not surprisingly, I had several contacts reach out and express hopeless feelings. I read about both scenarios on social media channels and I watched it on television interviews. This is where tenacity is required. Successful people are persistent, they overcome adverse conditions, they reach for more, and they are tenacious.

Tenacious people are not average; they accept failure and shortcomings as part of the risk. Average people never try hard enough, and neither Mitt Romney nor Barack Obama are average. Some people want to be average, and some may identify success with average results. If average is not your view of success, then you need tenacity.

Average is not a place or a label I want. What about you?

RULES OF GIVE

We've all heard that it is better to give than receive. Our lives are full of give and take, ups and downs, and excitement and boredom. Both our personal and professional lives may require us to give more than we take. This simple concept is what separates those who achieve from those who are stuck with a lifetime of poor choices, bad outcomes, and spiteful envy.

I believe most people encounter someone in their life who tells them that they can't. Someone may imply it, or may hit them with a verbal assault. On more than one occasion, I was told that I was no good, worthless, and never would amount to anything. This is the first rule of give—don't give in. If someone tells you that you are worthless, get away from that person now. You are better than that.

Persistence is the name of the game for those who are serious about making positive changes that stick. Too often, people stop pushing out of near-exhaustion or temporary disbelief in their capabilities. This is the second rule of give—don't give up. Your next opportunity is already waiting for you; don't give up now.

Sometimes people jump into endeavors halfheartedly. They push hard for a short period of time just to "test the water," and when they find out that nothing worth having comes easily, they start to look for excuses or reasons to blame someone else. Often they settle for the path of least resistance. This represents the third rule of give—you must give it all you've got.

Break a bad habit, a tradition, or a way of doing things—but don't ever break the rules of give.

CONSEQUENCES OF PERSISTENCE

Do you ever wonder if your efforts to change are working? Change your message, change yourself, or change your business, and people will notice. When you pivot, your network reacts. Paradoxical to your expectations, their reactions may not always be positive.

Positive people expect family, friends, and business associates to react positively to growth, change, and newfound success. Sadly, some percentage of their network may be troubled by this change—not by their choice and typically not their intentions (unless they are fleeing a destructive and inappropriate network) but because some people will not accept that others are pursuing or doing something they could never do themselves. Bear in mind they aren't incapable because they lack the skill, talent, or opportunity, but because they don't believe enough in themselves.

Since they don't believe, they don't try; because they don't try, they never get any results. They find it much easier to place blame and feel regret rather than pursue something that requires risk, passion, and dedication. They lack self-confidence and see only their burdens and failures instead of opportunities for change and success.

Time and time again, I hear stories of those who are envious of a friend's weight loss, job promotion, income, car, house, boat, wardrobe, shoes, hair, smile, and even cell phone! When your ability to tackle obstacles, face challenges, and remain disciplined in your pursuit pays off, some are not going to like it.

What can you do?

Embrace newfound friendships, stay focused, and always remain kind. Everything has a price tag, and positive change may mean new friends, a clearer and more direct focus, and a celebration of your accomplishments, all while never forgetting where you started. Don't dismiss your family, friends, and business associates, but remember that if they are in your network for the right reasons they'll be there congratulating you on positive change!

Otherwise, their loss may become a consequence of persistence.

CHAPTER SUMMARY

People may consider persistence to be an obsession, and perhaps for some it is. I believe persistence is a wildly fascinating topic that is paramount for both individual and business success. If you have a vision, dream, business plan, or strategy, you have to tackle it with persistence.

Many people like easy. They avoid conflict, hard work, and risk. Some of this may be human nature; it could be what separates leaders from followers. Of course not everyone can lead, and not everyone should try—and they don't.

It is hard for me to understand people who don't want more from their lives, their jobs, or their careers, but many do not. I've discovered this time and again in seminars that I have delivered. It is easy to spot those who are interested, engaged, and want more as compared to those who are simply occupying space and time.

Seth Godin wrote a book titled *Tribes*[2] that I found fascinatingly refreshing, thought provoking, and perhaps even intoxicating. If you are familiar with this book, perhaps you agree. Seth's work provided a lot of meaning, and it made me think about who is in my tribe and what type of follower he or she is. Sometimes we all follow—me, you, everyone. Being a follower doesn't indicate you are substandard, weak, or unable to lead. Followers are often brilliant and they are learning. Followers have interests in like products, goods, services, movements, culture, and more. Followers are as important as leaders, or maybe more so. Without followers there would be no purpose for a leader.

I'm mentioning followers, tribes, and leaders because they are a fundamental part of the function of those who succeed. I believe this because I view my network as predominately persistent people. Some have been very successful, some are strategizing on their next move, but they're all working hard. You see, persistent people are like-minded; otherwise they are completely turned off by the thought of persistence, confidence, focusing, pivoting, and acceleration.

Persistence is not for everyone, but I hope that persistence is for you. If you're reading this, chances are good that it is. Persistence is part of heart, not talent. Heart will trump talent—you can bet on it!

CHAPTER 10

RESULTS

Your time is limited, so don't waste it living someone else's life. Don't be trapped by dogma— which is living with the results of other people's thinking. Don't let the noise of others' opinions drown out your own inner voice. And most important, have the courage to follow your heart and intuition.

Steve Jobs[1]

Results develop from dreams, but only dreaming will not get you results. We can talk, dare to dream, and wait for the big break that may never come, or we can persistently push toward our goal to create the results we want. There is something about working hard and pushing the limits that makes people value those accomplishments more than those that come easily.

Today so many things tempt people to obtain something they may want or desire for free. There is something about free that is starting to signal untrustworthiness for many, and yet others flock to free with little or no thought about any potential consequences. They trust free. We have free memberships, free books, free sign-ups, free T-shirts, free ice cream, free soda, and sometimes free money. Are any of those things really free? Well, yes and no. Most of them come with some kind of string attached. All of them are striving for something—results.

Chances are great that if you're reading this book, you already know the results that you dream about will not come to you for free. What you desire is more than something that is obtainable for free. In the new marketplace there will be lots of free stuff, but the stuff that you value comes with a price. The price that you pay for making positive changes, dreaming big, assuming risk, and being persistent is far less than the price you would pay for staying stuck or living your life accepting less than your dream.

You want results, you want success, and you understand success is something that you define. It is different for everyone. Some achieve it while others do not, but one thing is certain: everyone who achieves it had the courage for the pursuit. That is what is so intoxicating about dreaming, believing, and achieving goals; it allows you to be you.

Success isn't about luck, gifts, or even about money. Success is about how you feel when you know you've given life everything you've got. You've failed, been burned, and been ridiculed and accused. Every time, you've faced it and moved on. You don't blame, cower, or envy others—you take it on the chin and then give one back. That's the difference between those who make it happen, and those who watch. That's results; that's success!

TOUGH DAYS

There are businesses that are doing fantastic, others that are struggling, and those that have gone out of business. There are individuals who are succeeding, growing, and achieving excellence, and there are individuals who are coming up short, falling behind, and feeling down. Businesses and individuals can blame this on many factors, but blame will not get you moving in the right direction.

Accept this—there will be tough days. Whether they are people who appear successful or those that do not, everyone faces challenges. On these days you need to dig deep and find ways to pick yourself up. Call a friend, discuss lessons learned with a colleague, or begin to search for future opportunities.

Not every day will be this tough. That is the best part of all. On good days, take the time to celebrate, enjoy, and feel pride.

Persistent people rise above the tough days. We call these people *successful.*

BLAMED FOR DISAPPOINTMENT

Everyone experiences disappointment. You didn't get the new job, your best client didn't renew your contract, or your last dining experience felt like a bad day at a three-day-old-sushi bar. Regardless of your level of success, everyone faces disappointment; how you manage it conditions your future.

There are several key factors to keep in mind. The first is that you must face the reality of the circumstances. Facing the reality is often the hardest part. In some cases, you own the responsibility. In other cases you may not, but you must carefully assess the decisions and choices that led up to the disappointing event.

The second factor to remember is that you can change it. You can choose to learn from the event, or disregard it by blaming someone else. Circumstances and situations vary, but in nearly all of them, you have choices.

But here is the most important factor of all: if you blame someone else, chances are good it will happen again.

Repetitive patterns of disappointment that are blamed on others often create a mind-set of resentment and victimization. Neither of those emotional traps will lead you to your success.

NO ONE TO BLAME

When the results are less than you expected, who do you blame?

There will always be circumstances beyond your control; there will be both good luck and bad luck. Successful people make the most of every situation; they seek positive outcomes even in the most trying and difficult times. They accept responsibility for outcomes and learn from mistakes.

Successful people never fail; to them, average is the opposite of success, not failure. They face outcomes from their choices, bravely confront risks, and have every right to take pride in the rewards. Successful people don't waste time with envy; they don't look for someone else to blame. They know that blame keeps people looking in the past, and that their success exists in the future.

Successful people know that one of their greatest strengths is accepting that there is no one *else* to blame.

HAPPINESS IS

A great friend sparked my curiosity by asking me about the definition of success. It seems to me that people often quickly associate their success, work, and social status with money.

MONEY IS IMPORTANT, BUT IT ISN'T NECESSARILY HAPPINESS.

Many people believe that money is their answer. Sure, in some cases having some amount of money can help ease a few of life's pains. There is less frustration in trying to pay bills, and maybe there are opportunities for a nice vacation, a new outfit or shoes, or even a nice gift for someone you care about. Money is important, but it isn't necessarily happiness.

Somehow I'm reminded of the childhood book *Happiness Is a Warm Puppy*, by Charles M. Schulz. Although today I couldn't tell you about the exact contents of this book, I remember having it as a child, and I believe that the message it tried to send was that happiness can mean many things. Simple things.

Back to my friend—he suggested that success is happiness. Since success has a very individual and perhaps personal definition, success is really about achieving happiness. After some thought, I have to tell you that I couldn't agree with him more.

Be happy!

REAL DEAL

People do strange things. Let's face it; we interact with people all the time who make us curious about what they think or what actions they take. This could quickly turn into a very deep discussion based upon opinions, experiences, and espoused values, but not necessarily the facts.

Occasionally I will encounter people who put down others when they have done something great or are finally getting on the right track. People are often critical of other people—very critical. Sadly, this may be rooted in their own insecurities or lackluster performances.

People notice when things change. When someone does something different or out of the ordinary, people will notice. When someone gets recognition for a job well done—yes, people notice. People who are on the move, are assertive, and make things happen tend to rattle the cages of those who are not.

The next time someone says something negative about another person's success, smile inside because you know the real deal!

WHATEVER IT TAKES

Most successful people work very hard. It's easy for the envious, jealous, and those with the victim mind-set to make excuses and cast blame about their own lack of success.

People with passion have purpose. They push forward constantly while measuring their progress against the desired end result. They evaluate against the goal, they change, adapt, and feel emotional satisfaction in small wins. They view setbacks or failures as temporary. They learn from them and improve. They are persistent.

While drive and determination are extremely important, do you know what the biggest difference between those who achieve their success and those who don't is?

Successful people are willing to do the things that others don't or won't.

UNDERESTIMATED SUCCESS

Failing to recognize the success you create can be an eye-opening experience. Occasionally we hear about the right product but at the wrong time. In other cases, we may find this to be true of people in workplaces or businesses. Sometimes it may be the "right skill or talent" but at a time when the business cannot fully utilize those qualities.

In many of these cases, people give up. They let go of product designs, brands, logos, and people, both professionally and personally. In some business situations, they may sell their rights, but when someone else makes it a huge success, they feel ripped off or shortchanged. They have underestimated the value or the potential of success.

Recognizing the immediate impact is painful, but that is nothing compared to the long-term value. What will it be worth in the future? What knowledge, skills, or abilities do you have that are valuable? What are the products, brands, or ideas you have that are underestimated, taken for granted, or simply considered dead ends?

There is an old idiom: "One man's trash is another man's treasure."

What have you underestimated?

BELIEF: THE PATHWAY TO SUCCESS

Confidence can be a significant factor in achieving the success that you dream about. The great thing about confidence is that it can be built, so if we need more, we can build more.

Belief in yourself or your capabilities can have a significant impact on your results. Your results may also be limited or conditioned by factors that hinder performance rather than enhance it. Here are three:

1. Action anxiety

2. Negative fantasies

3. Fear of separation

Confidence, belief, and reasonable risk all play a role. People who create their path to success also encounter those who are jealous or envious of their accomplishments. You should provide your own frame for your success; don't allow others to establish a frame for you. People who are less confident often try to limit the success of those around them.

Your success is within your reach. Make today the day you break through.

I believe—do you?

CHAPTER SUMMARY

They are what we are searching for, working hard for, risking for: results. Results can only be created through effort, taking chances, pushing hard, facing challenges, risking, dreaming, and believing. People who are persistent and have the ability to overcome disappointment, ridicule, and failure will become the most successful.

Results are sometimes feared; we may fear test results or feedback from our bosses or colleagues. Whenever we put forward effort, there will be some results. Whether the results are good, bad, or ugly, those who are successful realize that they need to face them. It is often challenging because when you have given it your best shot, you expect great results. Unfortunately this does not always happen.

THIS IS WHERE YOU FACE THE REALITY OF YOUR CIRCUMSTANCES OR SITUATION, AND MAKE A CONSCIOUS CHOICE TO EITHER REACH FOR MORE OR THROW IN THE TOWEL.

This is where you can really make a difference. Persistence plays a bigger role than perhaps previously recognized. This is where you face the reality of your circumstances or situation, and make a conscious choice to either reach for more or throw in the towel.

While there may be a time to stop, or a time to call enough, persistent people will typically only pivot toward their next move. Not every endeavor is right for every person. Sometimes it isn't the right time; other forces such as the government or economy can make the timing all wrong. You need careful evaluation as you explore your results. Excuses are useless, and if you cast blame, position yourself as the victim, or simply choose to ignore the reality of your results, the chances are good you will not obtain the results you are looking for.

So it comes down to how you use the results you've obtained. They are opportunities. Good or bad, how you manage the results you've achieved will condition your next move. Bad or undesirable results need to be carefully examined, evaluated for lessons learned, and then moved beyond. Good results need to be celebrated, evaluated for what led to the great achievement, and then built upon for increased confidence, positioning you for future success.

Both kinds of results, good or bad, have value, but you cannot dwell too much on either. Many people tend to remember and undesirably cling to the bad. On the other hand, we can become overconfident from good results, relax too much, and become complacent, lazy, and sloppy.

Use both kinds of results appropriately. Use them to your advantage. Explore opportunities, and most of all, create more results!

Dennis E. Gilbert

CHAPTER 11

ACCELERATE

Life is like a ten-speed bicycle. Most of us have gears we never use.

Charles M. Schulz[1]

Talking about it is easy. Doing it requires action. People on their way to a better path and a more rewarding future understand that they have to face tough obstacles, doubters, and sometimes ridicule. If you have accepted the concept of pivot, as put forward in earlier chapters, you next need to be prepared to accelerate. Just as the quote by Charles M. Schulz that opens this chapter reflects, many times we haven't capitalized on our ability to accelerate toward our goals. Fear, concern, and even confidence may lead to procrastination or hesitation, neither of which is consistent with people who are on the move. You can't just talk about it; you have to do it.

Having a dream is important. Dreams help supply the vision for your journey. However, being in a constant state of dreaming will not bring you closer to your goals. Your dreams and goals need to be big enough, lofty enough, and audacious enough to keep pulling you in, drawing you inch by inch and yard by yard closer toward your desired result.

WHEN YOU SEE THE KIND OF RESULTS YOU SEEK, IT BECOMES MORE ABOUT ACCELERATION.

There is something intoxicating about being fixed and focused on your goals while running toward your end result. Some may argue it is a marathon, but I believe it is more of a sprint. Checkpoints cause brief pauses while you compare results against previously developed timelines and milestones. When you see the kind of results you seek, it becomes more about acceleration.

Traveling at speed increases the risk, but when you know you are on target, speed allows you to surpass the competition. Survival in our world continues to be very competitive. Chances are great that in your desired field, occupation, or business, being early to the table will position you much better than being mid-packed or arriving late. Always remember that nothing worth having comes easily or without risk.

Sprinting at full speed allows you an opportunity to make a small mistake, bobble a bit, miss a turn, or miscalculate the necessary resources, but still be there early. This doesn't mean that you sprint with your eyes closed, or that you skip over or miss valuable opportunities. It does mean that when you are sprinting ahead of the competition you may be far enough ahead that you can afford to make an error or two, pick up those pieces, and still be in the front of the pack. Those who have mastered the art of the pivot recognize that it isn't over when you experience a setback or failure or when someone else says you are done. You are done when you stop looking forward and choose to live your life thinking only about what went wrong yesterday.

Acceleration means there isn't the time or the desire to keep looking back. The undesirable feelings back there really don't matter. Some of the past matters; it matters for reflection of self-improvement, confidence, and lessons learned. It doesn't matter for those who are not committed to their own success and attempt to sabotage yours—or for those who choose to view your success with envy, jealousy, or ridicule at missed attempts. You're on the move; the past is falling behind you at your rate of acceleration. Your peripheral vision is blurred, but what is in front of you is crystal clear.

SPEED SETS THE EXAMPLE, RAISES THE BAR, AND CREATES MOMENTUM.

Some may encourage you to slow down, be patient, and move at a more reasonable pace. Words of wisdom, maybe, but if you are not out of control, why wait? Patience is important, but when you know exactly where your next goal is, why wait? Speed sets the example, raises the bar, and creates momentum. Someone once told me that placing a nickel directly in front of a stopped train may stop it from moving forward, but a train running at speed will crush the nickel like it is not even there. Momentum is important; it may represent the silver bullet you've been hoping for. At a minimum it will set you apart from others who are too afraid to accelerate.

People often predict that someday they will embark on the journey that takes them where they dream of being. They visualize their success, but procrastinate their way through each day, then a week, then a month, a year, then two years, and then five. Suddenly it is too late; they've missed their window or have dramatically decreased their odds of success. If you are determined, persistent, and willing to pivot as required, it is time for acceleration. Don't talk about doing it one day. One day may never come. Make a conscious choice, and make today day one.

CHAPTER SUMMARY

Everyone has experienced acceleration: in a car, motorcycle, train, bus, or airplane. The pivot is critical, but acceleration will make the difference in your arrival time. Just like the train that crushes the nickel, momentum is hard to stop. Acceleration may not always feel completely safe. However, if there is an absence of fear, the goal, dream, or innovative idea may not be significant enough to draw you in and pull you toward your next achievement. Things that come easily become boring; dreaming big is energizing.

When will you start? You have to be courageous enough to put the pedal to the metal, throttle up, pin it, and hang on.

Today is the day you should start, because today someone will accomplish a goal, exceed a sales quota, or get a promotion. Someone else will receive a trademark, get a patent, or launch a new product, and another person will pay off some debt, buy a new car, or close on a mortgage.

I see a pattern here; do you? It's a great day to be someone.

Pivot and accelerate!

NOTES

CHAPTER 1

1. Winston Churchill. BrainyQuote.com, Xplore Inc, 2013.
    http://www.brainyquote.com/quotes/quotes/w/
    winstonchu138235.html, accessed December 8, 2013.

2. Jim Collins and Morten T. Hansen, *Great By Choice: Uncertainty, Chaos, and Luck—Why Some Thrive Despite Them All.* (New York: HarperCollins, 2011), 177.

CHAPTER 2

1. Alan Lakein. BrainyQuote.com, Xplore Inc, 2013. http://www.brainyquote.com/quotes/quotes/a/a lanlakein154655.html, accessed August 29, 2013.

2. "Alan Lakein," *Wikipedia,* last modified April 23, 2013, http://en.wikipedia.org/wiki/Alan_Lakein.

CHAPTER 3

1. Richard Branson. BrainyQuote.com, Xplore Inc, 2013. http://www.brainyquote.com/quotes/quotes/r/richardbra183468.html, accessed October 1, 2013.

2. Jim Collins and Morten T. Hansen, *Great By Choice: Uncertainty, Chaos, and Luck—Why Some Thrive Despite Them All.* (New York: HarperCollins, 2011), 177.

CHAPTER 4

1. Stephen Hawking. BrainyQuote.com, Xplore Inc, 2013. http://www.brainyquote.com/quotes/quotes/s/stephenhaw393342.html, accessed October 1, 2013.

CHAPTER 5

1. Eleanor Roosevelt. BrainyQuote.com, Xplore Inc, 2013. http://www.brainyquote.com/quotes/quotes/e/eleanorroo121157.html, accessed October 2, 2013.

CHAPTER 6

1.   Tony Robbins. BrainyQuote.com, Xplore Inc, 2013.
     http://www.brainyquote.com/quotes/quotes/t/t
     onyrobbin165101.html, accessed October 2, 2013.

CHAPTER 7

1.   Clint Eastwood. BrainyQuote.com, Xplore Inc, 2013.
     http://www.brainyquote.com/quotes/quotes/c/
     clinteastw122671.html, accessed October 2, 2013.

CHAPTER 8

1.   Henry Ford. BrainyQuote.com, Xplore Inc, 2013.
     http://www.brainyquote.com/quotes/quotes/h/
     henryford122817.html, accessed October 3, 2013.

CHAPTER 9

1. Ralph Bunche. BrainyQuote.com, Xplore Inc, 2013. http://www.brainyquote.com/quotes/quotes/r/r alphbunch392736.html, accessed October 8, 2013.

2. Seth Godin, *Tribes* (New York: Penguin Group, 2008).

CHAPTER 10

1. Steve Jobs. BrainyQuote.com, Xplore Inc, 2013. http://www.brainyquote.com/quotes/quotes/s/s tevejobs416854.html, accessed October 9, 2013.

CHAPTER 11

1. Charles M. Schulz. BrainyQuote.com, Xplore Inc, 2013. http://www.brainyquote.com/quotes/quotes/c/ charlesms189863.html, accessed October 23, 2013.

Dennis E. Gilbert

INDEX

G

H

T

Dennis E. Gilbert

ABOUT THE AUTHOR

Mr. Dennis E. Gilbert is the president of Appreciative Strategies, LLC, a human performance improvement training and consulting business. He combines his expertise in private, for-profit business management with his experience in the nonprofit educational sector to deliver outstanding results through consultation and training interventions. His extensive background in management and education is the culmination of over twenty-five years of experience with both for-profit businesses and nonprofit institutions of higher learning.

Dennis helps people and businesses discover and create their futures. He is a consultant, trainer, speaker, and author who is available for worldwide engagements.

For more information visit his website:

http://DennisEGilbert.com